Dedications

To my parents: my father, the greatest man I ever knew, and my mother, without whose support I could not have achieved anything in life; to the Rev. John J. Castelot, my friend and mentor growing up, who was the most intelligent person I could ever hope to meet, and who inspired me to teach and write; and to Anna, an amazing friend, beautiful soul, and the most talented person I have ever met.

And to the people in my life without whom I would never have found the courage and inspiration to write this book: Qixuan Fu, Maria and Dima, Steve Schiestel, Mike Arbet and Anastasia Orlina. True friends and wonderful people, one and all.

Contents

Every day I get up and look through the Forbes List of the richest people in America. If I'm not there, I go to work. – Robert Orben

Introduction

Beer and pizza – I thought those were the two major food groups when I was in college. And they made up a significant part of my budget! In those days, my "budget" was however much cash I had in my wallet or pockets at any given time. Of course, I also had other expenses vital to sustaining life: fast food, movie tickets, video games....

Eventually I graduated and discovered the wonderful world of rent and utilities, and then the real budgeting began. Or at least it *should* have begun. In college I had taken classes in Economics, World History, even Oceanography (that *really* came in handy working in Finance!). But there were no courses in personal finance. There also was no Internet, and no way for me to know how to manage my money – what little of it there was.

Fast forward a few years (ok, many years), and I found myself teaching Finance at one of the best universities in the country. I was teaching courses that were mainly about corporate finance, but I found that whenever I touched on *personal* finance, the number of people eagerly engaged (or awake!) skyrocketed. Even people who had looked like they were in a coma became conscious and were paying attention!

As I noticed this pattern happening more and more, I started asking students what they thought about my personal finance lectures. The feedback was incredible! They not only liked my practical and real-world approach to all aspects of finance, they told me they were learning things they couldn't seem to get anywhere else. They even laughed at my corny jokes!

But wait a minute...now there *were* courses in personal finance, this thing called the Internet *had* been invented and had been running for, oh about 20 years or so, and there were even tons of books out there about personal finance. Yet nearly all of my students told me they weren't getting the help they needed when it came to learning how to manage money.

Then I discovered what the problem was. It wasn't a lack of information, it was the lack of a *useful message*. There were and are books and websites out there with great advice and information about money and personal finance. But too many of them make it seem like a chore, and a painful one at that! Too many books over-emphasize sacrificing the present (and perhaps many years to come) for an unknown future. Successfully managing your money and building wealth can be hard work, but it doesn't have to be painful – it might even be fun!

So I decided to write this book – a light-hearted yet serious look at how to manage one of the most important resources you will have in building a comfortable and successful life for yourself: money. Even if parts of the book are not 100% applicable to your situation right now, they probably will be in the future. So hopefully this will be a guide for you not only today, but also as you build what is hopefully a happy and prosperous financial life!

"Explain to me again why enjoying life when
I retire is more important than enjoying life now."

Who needs this book? And if it's me, why do I need it?

Money – do you need it? Like it? Want it?

If you answered no to all of these questions, then I'm sorry, this book is not for you. But if you answered yes to even one...read on!

Of course we all need money at some point. Some of us (not me ☹) already have enough of it, maybe even all we'll ever need (if this is you, I'm happily accepting donations!). But even then, you'll need to know how to manage it and hold onto it.

For the rest of us... we also need to know how to manage and maintain it, but there is so much more to using this great tool called money – knowing how to use it can be the difference between a comfortable life and, well, turning life into a financial struggle.

This book can help anyone understand money better – what it is, how to manage it and make it grow. This version was specially written for college students and recent college grads, people aged, say, 17-25. I decided not to write a 'one-size-fits-all' book about finance, because, let's face it, how often does one size of anything really fit all? We all have very different needs, goals and circumstances in every stage of our lives.

That's not to say that if you are younger than 17 or older than 25 you won't get anything out of this version of the book. In fact, people of all ages can learn a great deal about money from this book – it could even change your life.

But why do you need **this** particular book? After all, aren't there already tons of books out there about money and finance? Books that range from telling you to get rich slowly all the way to those that promise to turn you into Warren Buffett overnight?

Of course! But in talking to literally hundreds of college-age people –
students and those in the working world – I found that people are not
getting enough of the *real, practical* help they want and need to
figure how to handle one of the most important tools and resources
you will have in life: money.

This book will cut through all the nonsense, hype, and frankly BS that
is all too common out there when it comes to teaching you about
money. It will give you easy to understand information you can use
today, in the *real world*! And it will speak to you as a real person, not
preach to you like a textbook would. It won't give you the false hope
of instant riches, but it also won't make you feel like you have to wait
for the next 60 years to have a solid, happy financial life. You can
start to build wealth today, and improve your financial life *right now*
– but it will probably take a little longer to get that first Porsche or sail
your yacht to Tahiti!

What I **can't** promise you:

- That you will be rich by next Tuesday (or next week, or
  probably even next year unless you already are rich!).

- That building a strong and solid financial life isn't hard work. It
  is, but it can be a lot more fun and interesting than you might
  think!

- That you will *ever* be rich – but I do believe that if you read
  this book, build a plan and stick to it, you have the greatest
  possible chance of reaching and exceeding your financial
  goals, both now and over the entire course of your life.

What I believe I **can** offer you:

- That if you follow the advice in this book, you will have a much
  better financial life.

- That if you are willing to learn a little bit and work at it, you can achieve your financial goals and dreams with my help.

So let's get started! I'm happy to help lead you down the path to financial freedom starting today!

How to use this book

Since this isn't a novel, you don't necessarily have to read it cover to cover. But if you're a beginner when it comes to finance, it's probably a good idea to just keep reading and go all the way to the end.

What if I already know a lot about personal finance?

That's ok, you can still get a lot out of this book. Unless you had a year-long internship with Warren Buffett, chances are high you can still learn a lot form this book even with an advanced level of financial knowledge.

If that's the case you'll probably want to skip around and only read the sections you're interested in learning more about. It can also be used as a reference guide as you build and improve your finances and investments. Plus, by buying this book and signing up for the **"Building Lifetime Wealth"** website (www.bldglifetimewealth.com), you will receive a discount on all my future books, many of which will feature more advanced financial strategies and techniques.

What if I don't really like reading and/or talking about money?

That's ok too; that's why I've tried to keep this book light and enjoyable. You too can use only the sections you are most interested in. As your finances get stronger and stronger, and as your life develops, you'll probably find more and more sections of the books will be of interest and help to you.

Money isn't the most important thing in life, but it's pretty close to oxygen on the "gotta have it scale" – Zig Ziglar

Introduction to Personal Finance

What is Personal Finance? How can this book teach me about it?

Personal Finance is the part of the field of Finance that relates to people rather than corporations (which is called Corporate Finance). Makes sense, right?

Put more simply, personal finance is how people manage their personal money. It can mean things like budgeting, planning, investing, and even making big purchases like cars or houses (or hopefully someday a yacht! One can always dream...).

Learning about personal finance is the way to make your money grow, last, and enable you to make some of those big purchases mentioned above. Of course, bad personal financial practices can make your money shrink, get you in too much debt, and lead you to a poor financial future...but that is what this book should help you avoid!

To teach you about personal finance, and to help you build a strong financial future, this book is divided into 4 sections, each of which will enable you to build on the knowledge you gain from the previous sections:

Learn – where you will read about the basics of money and finance, and see definitions of the terms that will be used throughout this book and in the real world.

Start – this will enable you to start budgeting your income and expenses, as well as begin to plan for the future.

Build – this section will help you build the foundation of your financial life. Any structure is only as strong as its foundation. A house made out of bricks has the solidity and strength of bricks – a house of cards has the strength of a playing card. Ok, it's a silly example, but it's true. Make your financial foundation have the strength of bricks rather than the jack of diamonds.

Grow – watching your money grow is the fun part! Through wise and well-planned investing, you can take your finances to the next level.

You keep talking about the future. Is this just another book telling me I have to sacrifice everything today to have money to spend 50 years from now?

No! On the one hand it's true that if you spend every penny you make as soon as you make it, you'll never have anything left for the future. But by starting to improve your financial life *now* you will also have more available to you *now*. You can start building wealth today, but you don't have to wait until you retire to start enjoying it!

Finance, like a lot of things in life, is a balancing act. As I said, you can't spend every penny/dollar/Euro/Drachma you get as soon as you get it. Well, you *could*, but that's not a good strategy for having a happy financial present or future.

The key is to balance enjoying life today, while building something that will enable you to enjoy your financial life even more as you go along. To get started with this, you need to create a budget, which we'll talk about later on in the book. But the point here is: don't get discouraged about trying to improve your financial life – it's not a matter of suffering today to benefit some unforeseeable future down the road somewhere. It doesn't have to be tedious, it doesn't have to be painful...in fact it shouldn't be either of those! It can be very enjoyable to watch your money grow and to know that by learning just a few key principles of finance, you can reap the benefits both today and tomorrow!

SECTION I - LEARN

© 1996 Ted Goff

"There's nothing wrong with your personal finance software. You just don't have any money."

Money – what exactly is it?

In the previous section, I asked whether you like, need or want money. Yes, I know: pretty stupid questions!

Of course you know what it is; of course you need, like and want it! Ever seen the movie *Idiocracy*? One of the lead characters, the wonderfully named Frito Pendejo (look up the meaning of "pendejo" if you don't already know it), superbly played by Dax Shepard, keeps repeating "I *like* money" many times throughout the movie, as if he's the only one who does.

Actually there's more to the concept of money than you might think. It's more that the "available credit" left on your credit card, or the crumpled bills in your pocket, or the penny you just stepped over without bending down to pick up because, well, it's only a penny! (more on *that* later in the book).

Money is many things, and we'll talk about a lot of aspects of what money is, but mainly, for you, money is both a **tool** and a **resource**. A tool is just an object you use to do something you couldn't do (or couldn't do as well) without it. You could probably hammer a nail into a board without a hammer, but it's a lot easier if you use one. A car is a tool too – if you live 3-4 miles from work and need to get there in the next 10 minutes, you're almost certainly not going to get there without using the very valuable tool known as your car!

Money is a kind of a tool. It's something you can use to enable you to do something else. It allows you to obtain the things that will make your life easier, or in some cases, that you have to have to do the things you want or need to do in life. I've also described money as a resource; a resource is very much like a tool. Here's a few ways merriam-webster.com defines a resource:

- a source of supply or support: an available means

- a natural feature or phenomenon that enhances the quality of human life
- something to which one has recourse in difficulty

Both tools and resources allow you to use one thing to do something else. But a resource can also enhance the quality of life, help you out of difficulties...

So why define money this way? Because a lot of people have misconceptions about money, what it is, why you should want it, and frankly money can have a rather bad reputation at times! I'm sure you've heard the saying "money is the root of all evil". Well of course it isn't, but it's certainly true that people often do evil things to get it. And they often do evil things with it.

But there's nothing evil about money, and there is nothing wrong with trying to have it and make your supply of it grow. Now, if you do something illegal, unethical, immoral, something that hurts someone else, or is just plain wrong with it, that is most likely evil. But if you do, it's not money's fault – it's your fault! And you absolutely should not even think about doing any of those things with money, or in able to get money. In the end you will rarely profit from it (it will catch up to you), and in fact you'll probably end up with far less than you otherwise would.

By earning money and learning how to make it grow, you're building up the tools and resources you need to survive, to have a better life, buy a car to get to work in, travel, enjoy more leisure activities... You can, and absolutely should, do this in a way that is legal, ethical, moral, etc.. Given this, and by looking at money as a resource and tool, it's hard to see what is evil about wanting and needing to have it!

So it looks like we've answered the first question from the beginning of this section: do you need money? Yes! As for whether you like it or want it, that's for you to decide! But pursuing a better financial future, which involves building a supply of that necessary tool and resource known as money...it's important, it's worthwhile, and it's necessary.

In the next chapter, I'll tell you more about the nature of money, because I think it's important to know as much about it so that you can make the best decisions in managing it. But I'd like to end this chapter with a little non-financial advice when it comes to money.

> *Money frees you from doing things you dislike. Since I dislike doing nearly everything, money is handy.* – Groucho Marx

During my career, I've worked with people ranging from billionaires, business owners, professional athletes, musicians and corporate executives, to factory workers, people of very ordinary means, and people struggling to pay next month's rent. Looking back at my experiences helping these people, I noticed a pattern, or I should say a *lack* of a pattern: how happy or unhappy these people seemed to be in life had nothing to do with how much money they had.

Yes, I've heard that trite saying "money can't buy happiness", and no, I'm not trying to convey these cute little sayings to you in this book. What I'm saying is that while building a solid financial future is extremely important, it shouldn't consume your whole life. Some of the extremely wealthy people I have worked with have been among the happiest people I ever met, and some among the most miserable. I've worked with people who have had little-to-no money yet couldn't be happier, and people who work away the whole lives just to survive from one week to the next.

The point is, there's a middle ground, a balance between working and living, earning and spending. I've seen too many people whose every waking moment is an endless pursuit of squeezing every penny out of their career. If that's what truly makes you happy, do it. But for the rest of us, we need to find a place in between constant work and not doing enough to earn a living. Absolutely work, earn, make your money grow, but make time for yourself and the people you care about…and spend some of the money you make too!

If you follow the things you learn in this book, you will be better equipped to meet your financial needs and goals, which hopefully includes enjoying the money you work hard to make. Many of you reading this book are in college or maybe just graduated. If so, you have your whole life ahead of you – make it a good one!

Money is not the most important thing in life. Love is. Fortunately I love money – Jackie Mason

More about Money and a bit about classic Finance

So now I want to tell you a little bit more about the nature of money, as well as give you a few insights into the world of classic Finance. But not too much – this isn't a textbook!

Last chapter I listed a few things we think of as "money": banknotes (dollar bills), coins; even available credit on a credit card could be considered money of a sort. Many, many years ago, salt was commonly used to buy goods and services – so is salt money too? It could be, if someone was willing to accept it from you as payment for something.

But before you break out the salt shaker and head to the store, just know that salt was a form of currency at a time when it was a rare commodity. Since there's probably some on your kitchen table, it's not exactly rare anymore.

Money, in its purest definition, is a medium of exchange. That is, it's something that is generally accepted as a means of payment for goods and services by a society. Put another way, it's something that someone else will take from you for something you want to buy from them...clothes, groceries, or a service such as a haircut.

Spending money, or just making your food taste better?

But in the modern world, it's necessary to have some *standard* medium of exchange, something that everyone can agree to take in exchange for whatever it is their selling: and that's where banknotes (bills) and coins have come into play.

So instead of carrying around a variety of things that people might want in exchange for products they're selling or services they're offering, we just carry around a wallet full of paper bills, a pocket full of coins, or a credit card or two! Whew! Is that all I need to know about money now?

Well, that isn't everything money is: bills and coins are "currency"; a part of what the concept of money is all about. It's a very important part, certainly, but there is something else you need to know about money before we move onto the good stuff, which is how to make your money *work for you*. And that is: money changes over time.

I'm not talking about the banknotes, bills and coins that we usually think of as money. Of course that changes over time, new bills are designed, coins with different fronts and backs are minted...many countries have even switched to plastic banknotes. No, that's not the change I'm talking about: what I'm saying is that the **value** of money is always changing; it's value to you and how much you can buy with it.

Here are a few examples: if I told you I will either give you $100 today, or $100 two years from today, which would you choose? Without even knowing what I'm getting at yet, you'd rather have the money today, right? Why wait 2 years, when you can spend the money this afternoon?! Yes, that's one reason you'd rather have money now rather than later, and here's another:

Say you found an investment opportunity where you could make a 10% return (profit) each year over the next 2 years with the $100 I just offered you. Now the choice of whether to take the money today or later has another dimension, one that makes it a much more obvious choice. If you invest in this opportunity today, two years from now you would have $121 (your $100 would earn 10%, or $10, in the first year, after which you have $110. Moving a year ahead, that $110 would then earn another year's return of 10%, which is $11, as $110 times 10% = $11. Add that to the $110 you started year 2 with, and now you have $121). So the second choice, to take $100 in 2 years, has obviously become the wrong one, since by investing right away you would have $21 more in the future than what I offered you.

This is one example of how the **time value of money** can work for you. I'm not going to go too deeply into the concept, because numerous chapters of finance textbooks are often devoted to "time value of money". Why I'm bringing this up is that it's a very important concept for you to have a working knowledge of – enough of an understanding of it to make better financial decisions.

So let's go back to the example we've been using in this chapter. With the opportunity to make a 10% every year for 2 years, the choice of when to take the $100 became obvious. But what if the second choice was to take $125 two years from today instead of just $100. Now suddenly *that* looks like the better option. From a financial standpoint, it would be.

These of course are very hypothetical examples. I'm sorry, but I'm not going to offer to just give you $100 now or 2 years from today. Nor is it likely any stranger on the street will either. But why these examples are potentially real is that you might make investments where different amounts of money may be available at different points in the future. For various reasons, you will likely have the possibility of different *cash flows*, money coming in and out of your personal wealth, at many different times in the future.

So you need to see that the value of money is constantly changing, rather than just staying the same throughout time. Yes, you can put a dollar bill on a table and watch it all day: it won't change, grow, shrink, talk, walk away (if you see it doing any of those things, let me know...there are other types of books I can recommend for you!)

But it's changing nonetheless – not physically, but in its value to you! If it's just sitting there, it's actually *losing* its value, because you could be investing it, paying down debt with it…. any number of things that will make its value to you more in the future than it is worth today.

So given the above examples, we can say that *interest rates* affect the value of money, or more specifically the time value of money. Because money you have today can grow, the same amount of money in the future (say, the $100 in the first example) is worth less to you in the future that it is now. And because you can continue (in theory) to earn more and more interest on that money, the further out in the future you go, the less that given future amount of money is worth to you today as well.

If you can remember this basic concept, that the value of money changes over time, it will put your farther ahead, financial knowledge-wise, than the vast majority of people you're likely to meet. And it should drive all of your financial decisions – not necessarily in a mathematical sense (you don't have to compute the last expected detail of every transaction you contemplate in advance), but rather in the way you think about spending and investing money.

There's another factor that's affects the value of money over time, and I promise I'll only spend a few sentences on it: inflation. Inflation makes the spending power of money shrink, for reasons I'll leave to an economics textbook.

> *Inflation is when you pay fifteen dollars for the ten-dollar haircut you used to get for five dollars when you had hair. – Sam Ewing*

Here's what you need to know about inflation: if you let money sit idle, and not make any kind of a return on it, its spending power gets less and less over time. If, for example, the rate of inflation is 2%, and you are not making at least a 2% return on your investments, you're not losing actual money, you're losing **buying power**. Keep that in mind if you become too afraid of risk and are earning very little reward on your investments. You'll see why this is important when we get to the Investments section of the book.

Buying Power

Buying power, simply, is how much power your money has to buy things, measured over time.

I first become aware of the effects of buying power at a time when I was trying to save money – I was buying a lot of boxed pasta. A box of spaghetti cost $1, and the price never seemed to change; it seemed a reliable amount to put into my budget.

But then one week I noticed my usual box of spaghetti cost $1.20! Ok, not a huge budget-buster, but still, a 20% increase in price?! When there was supposedly no inflation?

This is how changes in buying power works: Instead of the 20% inflation on the above box of pasta, let's look at a much more modest rate of 2% annually. Inflation reduces the value of money, and thus it's buying power. So here's what happens to $1 after inflation does it's thing: After 1 year, that $1 is worth 2% less, bringing its value down to 98 cents (from the perspective of our starting year). Here's a look at how it's value gets even less over time:

Years:	1	2	5	10
Value:	$0.98	$0.96	$0.90	$0.82

And here's what happens to the price of our box of pasta with 2% annual inflation.

Years:	1	2	5	10
Price:	$1.02	$1.04	$1.10	$1.22

For now, if you can keep in mind that you have to be aware of how the value of money to you changes over time, you're ready to move forward in building a much better financial future!

Section 2 – START

"So far, so good — I've got our budget all balanced except for food, clothing, and shelter!"

Budgeting

Do you know how much money you have available to spend *right now*? How much you need for rent or a car payment, for entertainment, and yes, maybe even for a burger or a pizza (and perhaps your beverage of choice)? Or do you use the "cash in the wallet" technique (whatever cash is in my wallet – that's how much I have to spend) for knowing your spending power at any given moment?

A budget can help you answer these questions, and also let you get the most out of your hard-earned dollars. Maybe your income is hardly earned rather than hard-earned, but once you've worked for your money, it's time to start getting your money to work for you! We'll look at how to really ramp this up when we talk about investments, but for now, let's at least make sure you know where your money is going when it's, ah, going.

Read any book on personal finance (but you're reading this book, so you don't need to read another personal finance book!), and they'll tell you the same thing: you need to have a *written* budget. Unless you have a photographic memory, it's a very good idea. When I was in college, I could count the number of my fellow students who actually did this on one hand...and have 5 fingers left over (for you non-math majors, that's, uh, none).

But that doesn't mean it isn't a great idea – it is. The good news is you don't have to draw up a budget covering every minute detail of everything you expect to happen for the next 5 years – you're not a corporation!

I actually did my first budget when I was a junior in college. I was tired of not knowing where my money was going and of feeling like I always had less of it than I thought. In fact, toward the end of each month, I never seemed to have any of it at all!

So I decided to write down where my money was coming from, and where I expected it to go. I decided to do a 1 month budget, and see how it worked. I took out a sheet of paper, and near the top I wrote "Income". Unfortunately there wasn't a lot to write under this heading, but I had a job where I got paid weekly on Fridays, so I multiplied my paycheck by 4 (there were 4 Fridays that month), and that was my Income for the month. I wrote that number next to Income.

A little further down, I wrote "Expenses". The good news back then was that although I didn't have much income, I didn't have too many bills to pay either. I decided only to write down the expenses I absolutely had to pay, as the point was to see how much money I had leftover to spend. I only had three items to write under expenses at that time: Rent (which wasn't much since I was renting a room in a house), Car Payment (which also wasn't much, because I didn't have much of a car), and Car Insurance (really? I actually had to insure that piece of crap?? Yes, replied the State government).

It's easy to meet expenses – everywhere you go, there they are -
Anonymous

So adding up these three items gave me my total Expenses, at least the expenses I was obligated to pay. At the bottom of the page I wrote "Spending Money" (later I changed this to Net Income, but more on that later). Now, for the very intricate part ☺: I took the Income number, subtracted the Expenses number, and voila, there was my spending money for the month! I divided this number by 4, and that was how much I had left for general spending each week. It would have been great if I had been able to put aside some of this total for other purposes, but it was a start on the road to improving my finances, and I was proud of it.

My first budget was finished and on paper, and the whole operation took, oh, 2, maybe 3, minutes (It took longer to write about it than actually do it!). And it helped. I had more money at the end of that month than I had at the end of a month in a long time. I even had some money left over after doing a little celebrating, so I carried it forward to the next month. Eventually I decided to save (and later invest) some of this extra amount, but we will talk about that a little later.

I did a simple paper budget like the one I just described for about a year and a half, and I was amazed at how much better my financial situation was. I wasn't rich, but I also wasn't puzzled all the time as to where my money was going and why I always seemed to have less than I thought. It was the first step to gaining control of my finances, and gaining control of my money rather than it controlling me.

The Envelope method

Fortunately, after a while I started having more and more "left over" cash at the end of the month from my new budgeting program. There wasn't a need any more to carry any of it over into next month's budget to *spend*, so I had to decide what to do with it. As there were several things I wanted to save for, and I hadn't yet discovered the wonderful world of spreadsheets, I came up with an idea: I grabbed a bunch of envelopes, and on each one I wrote one of the things I wanted to save for. I had envelopes for Savings, Investments, Travel, Car Repairs (this envelope saw a lot of action coming and going), House fund (for a down payment on a house someday), and since I liked to go to the casino from time to time, I even had an envelope labelled Casino (hey, it's a lot better than taking money from the Savings envelope to gamble with!).

Every week, I would take whatever cash I had left over, and put some in each of the envelopes. When the Savings envelope had $25 or so in it, I ran it up to the bank. When I had $1000 in the Investing envelope, I opened my first investment account. You get the idea. It's pretty simple, but it works.

Stuff I really can't afford and really don't need but I'm going to buy anyway

Now that we are moving towards being less and less of a cash-based society, this method may not work for as many people as it would have a few years ago. That's ok – you can just keep all of your funds in a bank account, and write how much is allocated for each purpose on a piece of paper. I highly recommend doing this, though it's much easier in Excel – I'll talk more about this in the section below.

Taking budgeting to the next level

Maybe the simple monthly paper budget is as far as you want to ever go with budgeting. That's fine – the good news is it's easy to do, takes virtually no time to create and maintain, and it will help you to at least see where your money is coming from and where it is going. If that's all you ever do when it comes to making a budget, you have at least made a major step toward having a better financial life.

But if you want to take budgeting to the next level, and have a lot more control over spending, saving and investing (see the chapters on the last 2 – I figured nobody needed help *spending* money!), then you might want to put your budget on Microsoft Excel.

As I mentioned earlier, I did the simple monthly paper budget for about a year and a half. At that time, I was working for a company that had just bought a new computer system, and they wanted someone to become their expert in this program that was called

Lotus 1-2-3. It was a precursor to Excel, and at that time nobody knew what to do with it. So I read a little bit of the book on Lotus that came with the new computers, and I started toying around on some spreadsheets. Actually, while Lotus 1-2-3 seems like a dinosaur now, it was a tremendous breakthrough at the time. It greatly simplified things for my company, and wound up making a huge difference in my life.

So I took my simple 4-line-item budget, and put it on a spreadsheet. OK, it looked nice, but what difference did it really make? Well, none at first, except it made things a bit easier when changes needed to be made. No need to re-calculate anything, the spreadsheet did it automatically.

Where the real difference came into play was when I started having more than just 4 entries in my budget. Soon thereafter I got my own apartment, and the line-items grew – unfortunately all on the Expenses side! But then I realized how I could make the budget work for me on the positive side too. I had already started putting money into a savings account, which was a lot more worthwhile then than it is today: savings accounts were paying 4-5% interest a year rather than the 0-1% they are paying now! I also started reading about investing, and I wanted to give it a try. I discovered my budget could do a lot more than just tell me how much I could spend each week – it showed me how I could improve all aspects of my financial life.

The first thing I did, once I decided to expand my budgeting using a spreadsheet, was to make it dynamic (changeable) rather than static (rarely updated). What I mean by that is the budget would change along with all of my changing circumstances – in fact it wound up being changed numerous times each month. I'm not saying you need to do that: a more static spreadsheet can still be a great one, and that might be how you prefer to run it. Since I have always been interested in numbers and finance, I didn't mind working with the spreadsheet so often.

The first change I made was to move the Net Income section from the bottom of the sheet to the top, and I changed the name to simply "Net", because now I wanted incoming and outgoing cash to balance. Then I changed "Expenses" to "Spending", because I wanted this to include not only bills I had to pay, but ways I was going to spend or allocate fund to either my present (daily spending) or my future (savings, investments, etc.).

The next step was set a weekly spending budget for myself, a sort of budget within the budget. At first, I just picked a number based on what I felt was a reasonable number, multiplied it by 4 (4 weeks in a month), and created a row in the spreadsheet simply labelled Weekly Spending (I shortened it to W to not confuse it with the Spending category). But after a while, I decided I wanted to break it down even further, so I created a new tab in my Budget spreadsheet called Weekly. Here I broke down each of the things I found myself spending money out of my wallet on in the course of a week, each with its own separate row: Gas, Groceries, Eating Out...you can make this as broad or narrow as you want. You might want to set up a row for things like Snacks, Entertainment, Bar...who knows, maybe you're a big pizza fan and want to have a row labelled Pizza! The beauty of this approach is you can customize it any way you want, with as few or as many entries as you want.

I also created new rows for other things I wanted to spend money that were not considered normal weekly spending, or that really weren't what you would think of as spending at all. I had a row for money I planned to send to my investment account, and a number of blank rows for anything else that might want to come up. Say I wanted to buy a new television or computer in about 6 months. Or maybe I wanted to take a trip someplace warm in December. Those items would go in the budget as well.

Before I go any further, I want to point out something I learned about Excel when teaching a class in it: the only way to actually learn how to use it is by actually using it! So for those that want to see what it is I'm talking about, there are a few budget templates on my website, bldglifetimewealth.com, including the ones I talk about in this chapter. Enjoy!

Back to budgeting. As my financial life got more and more complex, I decided to project my budget out for the next 12 months. That way I could see if there were any special expenses coming up that required a change in my spending (I now project out 2 years, though I doubt many other people would want to do that). How do you know what is going to happen in the next 12 months? Well, of course, you don't! Everything looking ahead is just an estimate, a way to give you advance warning of something that might need your attention.

So that's how my own personal budget has progressed over the years, made much easier through the power of Excel. Why did I go into such detail? I didn't do it to bore you with stories of my life, but to show you how your own budget, and in fact your entire financial life, will likely change and evolve as you get older and your life becomes more complex. A good budget can adapt to all of these life changes, but starting simple can still make a huge difference.

Getting started creating a budget

Whether you want to start simple or complex, do yourself a huge favor: just start! Maybe you would like to start simple, see how it goes, and then progress to a more complex budget? Not a bad idea at all! In fact, a great idea if you are new to the world of budgeting and your financial life isn't too complicated yet.

I won't go over the details of how to create a simple paper budget again, because it was all explained about 2-3 pages ago. The point is to separate income from expenses, list what is certain (paycheck under income, bills you *have* to pay under expenses), subtract expenses from income, and there is your surplus for the month (or whatever time period you decide to make a budget for).

Simple doesn't have to mean on paper only; Excel is very handy for creating extremely simple budgets as well. Not very experienced or comfortable using Excel? Here's another piece of advice I can't recommend strongly enough: learn it!! It will make your life easier in many ways, and be a huge boost to your future employability. If taking a class isn't an option, pick up a copy of Excel for Dummies. No, you're not a dummy if you don't know Excel, but the "for Dummies" book series is generally outstanding, and is a great way to start learning so many subjects. It's well worth the money, trust me!

So, if you've decided to start with a bit of a more complex budget, or you're ready to graduate from simple to complex, you will definitely want to use Excel. To start building your New & Improved Budget, the general financial principle is no different than for a simple budget: Income – Expenses = what you have left over to do other things with (in corporate finance it's Income = Revenue – Expenses, but as I said before, you're not a corporation! You can call the categories whatever you want; the principle is the same).

Before moving on from our discussion on budgeting, there are a few more things I'd like to tell you. For one thing, I want to point out that the purpose of a **weekly** budget if you choose to create one isn't to straight-jacket your spending. It's just to get a better idea of how much you might want to spend weekly on various items and activities. Say you want to go to a concert, you've already spent the amount you've allocated for Entertainment, but you haven't spent the amount next to Bar. Does that mean you have to skip the concert and go to the bar? Only if you want to! Or you can move some money from Bar to Entertainment – the point is to be flexible without overspending in general.

Some people might feel the need to control every penny of their spending, and it you're one of those people, then do it! This type of budget allows you the flexibility to make it as strict or loose as you want, to suit your needs, your lifestyle, your mentality. There's no right or wrong, as long as the budget is helping you get your money under control. If it isn't, you might want to consider tightening it up a bit. It's your money, your budget, your life...use it as you see best!

Planning

Here comes another cute little saying for you; I'm sure you've heard it at some point in your life: "Those who fail to plan, plan to fail". I hate trite sayings like that! But...while I won't go so far as to say this one is completely right, there's a lot of truth in it: you need a plan. And since this is a book about Finance, my strong advice is to come up with a *financial plan*.

Fortunately this is not as hard, tedious, or boring as it might seem. You don't have to try to outwrite War and Peace; your financial plan can be as long or short as you want it to be. In fact, it might just be a few sentences. It's really up to you, your mindset, and your character: if you're they type of person who likes to spell out every minute detail of their life, then write that kind of financial plan. If you prefer short and sweet, do it that way. There is no right or wrong, good or bad....except not having *some* kind of plan: that's not so good.

Here's another bit of pretty firm advice on the subject of financial planning: **write it down.** You will need something to look at from time to time to make sure you are staying on track. Unfortunately memorizing it will not be good enough, trust me. Write it, type it, carve it into marble if you want to (no wait, you want to revise it from time to time, so no marble), but make it something you can actually see. Do yourself a favor: put it on paper (who has enough marble lying around anyway?).

Here's something else I'm going to be firm about: **take it seriously.** Even if it's just a couple sentences, your plan is a sort of road map for where you want to wind up being in your financial life. It can have detailed instructions on every twist and turn you think you will need to make to reach your financial destination, or it might just list the destination itself. Again, it's up to you and to whatever you find most useful.

At a minimum, your plan will need to contain where you want to eventually wind up in your financial life. What are your ultimate goals? What kind of lifestyle do you want to have when you retire? What about your lifestyle before that (as in, right now)?

Investments and Financial Planning

"If you had taken tomorrow's advice yesterday, you'd be rich today!"

Here are the areas I recommend addressing when it comes to writing down your financial plan. Again, depending on your nature as a person, you might be able to address each with 1 sentence, a few bulletpoints, a paragraph or two, or a page or more. There is no right or wrong; what matters is what **you** find to be most useful:

Ultimate Goals: Here you can list everything you want to have and achieve at some point in your life. And it doesn't even need to be all *that* realistic, though you shouldn't list anything that is pretty much impossible. You can list your dreams, but if it's something you have absolutely zero chance of accomplishing in life, I'd leave it off. Examples of what I would **not** include in this section (or any other section): "I would like to own a fleet of 8 megayachts", or, "I would like to purchase New Zealand". But you could write something like: "I would like to own my own yacht someday". You may or may not achieve it, but at least it's in the realm of possibility. Think big, dream, but only put things in this section that there is even a remote possibility of accomplishing.

Retirement Goals: In this section, it can be helpful to write down the kind of lifestyle you want to have when you eventually retire. You don't need to know the exact amount you want to have in your account the day you retire, or the exact amount you will want to spend every month in retirement. But there are a few things you should think about (see the Retirement chapter for more on this):

- Where do you think you would like to live when you retire? It might be a simple as writing "Someplace warm", or "Near the ocean or a lake", or even someplace very specific such as "Albuquerque, New Mexico". And it could possibly change over time, but just write down your current thoughts of where you might like to retire. It may seem unrealistic, but it's always good to know what direction you want to take with your life. If you don't know where you are headed, how will you ever get to where you want to be?!

- Would you like to live in a house when you are retired, or would a condo or apartment be good enough for you? Again, you probably don't have a 100% clear picture of where you want to be living 40 or so years from now, but if you really can't see living in a condo or apartment when you retire, write something like "I would like to have my own house in my retirement years". Some people don't want to go through the trouble of upkeeping a big house (or wouldn't want to pay someone else to do it), so for them, a condo or apartment might be good enough. Write that down if you think it will be helpful.

- Do you expect to live a lavish lifestyle, or will you be content with living modestly? Do you want to travel a lot when you are retired, or spend most of your days fishing/shopping/eating...? Again, this could all very well change over the course of your life, but I really believe it's important to have goals, even if those goals change over the course of time. Examples of what you might write in this section are:

- o "I would like to take 2 major trips per year to out-of-the-way places in the world" (I had a client who was not super-rich and managed to do this well into his 80s).
- o "I want to lead a quiet life in retirement, and don't care at all about international travel"
- o "I want to be able to fish and play golf 5 times per week".
- o "I want to be able to eat at every expensive restaurant in town several times per week"
- o "I need to be able to visit family and friends across the country whenever I want to"

Things I can do to reach my goals: This section can be pretty generic. You might list things like opening an IRA, maintaining an investment

account (continuing to learn more about investing is also a good step to list if you are so inclined), maximizing your 401k contribution at work, etc. A lot of detail is not necessary in this section.

Source/Author unknown

Short-term Plans: These are things you can start doing <u>now</u> to help build toward your long-term and ultimate goals. The rest of this book will be devoted to things you can start doing in this regard, so you might want to finish the book before finishing this section of the plan. More on this as we go.

That's it. Or at least, that's it for now. You will want to revisit your plan periodically – at least once a year, though I recommend looking at it, and revising it if necessary, at least once every 3 months, or whenever a significant event takes place in your life.

You'll be surprised at how having something like this down on paper can help you focus your financial efforts, and even improve your financial situation over time!

Please also see the Building Lifetime Wealth website for more on how your Financial Plan can be put into practice.

SECTION III – BUILD

SAVING

Now you've reached the section of the book where you can learn about building actual wealth. Though the rest of the book is devoted to helping you grow your money, you first need a build a bit of money to work with. Then I'll show you how to keep it growing!

Even people with a casual knowledge of American history can tell you that Benjamin Franklin was a pretty smart guy. He was instrumental in harnessing the power of electricity, he was a key contributor to the drafting of the U.S. Constitution, and he invented the $100 bill. Ok, he didn't invent the $100 bill, but his face is on it, so he must have been doing something right!

Actually he was an extremely smart man. But he was also the guy who said "a penny saved is a penny earned". Is there any more boring quote in the world of finance, or any other world?? I can't think of one! I'd rather be out spending "Bens" than taking his advice and putting pennies into a piggy bank!

It may be a boring saying, but old Ben was right: saving money is a good idea; in fact, it's necessary. But it doesn't have to be a boring concept!

When I was in college, saving meant having enough money to be able to afford to go to a party that coming weekend (at least it did to me). When you're young, it's hard to think about saving. Spending is a lot more fun!

So, the trick is not to *think* of saving as socking coins away in a jar, or putting a few occasional dollars in a savings account...I want you to get away thinking of saving as boring or some sort of sacrifice. You need to save money, but I'd like you to think of it as BUILDING WEALTH. Because that's what you're doing. And you can start now!

This is how I recommend approaching starting to build your wealth:

- Have a line item in your budget (that hopefully you created after reading the last section!) called "My Wealth" (you can call it whatever you want; this is just a suggestion). **Create a good balance in your budget between having enough spending money to enjoy life and do things with your friends,** and allocating the rest of what you have left over every month to your Wealth Account.

- Save all of your coins: don't spend any of them! Put them in a jar, all of them.

- If you never use cash, but rather use your debit card for most purchases, see if your bank has a feature where they round up purchases to the nearest dollar, and deposit this extra amount into a savings account. If they do, **use it!!!**

- Build a War Chest.

Wealth Account

Actually, you will probably have several accounts in your lifetime that will house and enable your wealth to grow. I would recommend starting by putting the initial amount you start to set aside for wealth into your regular bank account (even if it is a checking account making no interest). This will also have the benefit of giving you a little bit of a cushion if some unforeseen bill or expense arises.

Since money in a regular bank account makes little-to-no interest, I wouldn't keep too much extra in there. I'd say $500 to $1000 at the most. Set a number you feel is right for you. Maybe it's as low as $100, or as high as $5000. I'd recommend a fairly low number ($500 is plenty to start). But base it on what you are most comfortable with.

When you have your initial bank account cushion, as I call it, now it's time to start to build an investment account. Go online and look at the different brokerage accounts available (the big ones are eTrade, Charles Schwab and Fidelity, but there are many others). An app such as Robinhood might also work. Find one with the features you think you will like best, and one that doesn't have too high of a minimum initial account deposit (unless you've already saved up a lot, in which case it doesn't matter). Now, instead of letting the amount you allocate to building wealth pile up in a bank account, send it to your new brokerage account.

You can start to build a decent investment account with as little as $1000, though you'll need more than this to be properly diversified. See the following section on Investments for how to build the type of account that will propel you towards accomplishing your financial needs and goals in life!

Coins

OK, didn't I just say, a short while ago, that putting pennies into a piggy bank was boring? Do they even make piggy banks anymore? Well personally, I don't find watching a large jar fill up with my coins that are adding to my wealth all that boring! It's not like you have to sit there and stare at it! You put a few coins in it every day, and it grows. I like that feeling.

What you do is (pay close attention, this is *very* complicated!): get a large jar of some sort, preferably one that is clear so that you can see into it. Then, whenever you get coins from whatever source: in change, or you find one on the sidewalk (yes, bend down and pick it up, it's good exercise!), you put it in the jar! See, I told you it was complicated!

The other thing that differentiates my coins suggestion from the "penny saved is a penny earned" saying is that I'm not suggesting you pinch every penny and not spend it: I'm saying put change you receive from things you pay for with cash in the savings jar. You can spend and save at the same time!

No, there is nothing even remotely revolutionary about saving change. People have been doing it since coins were invented. But the fact that I find so many coins on sidewalks tells me someone out there doesn't want their change. Well I do! And I recommend you to want it too.

I actually do like watching my change jar fill up. When it does, I take the coins to the bank, deposit them, and add the money to my investment account. No, an extra penny here and there will not make you rich, but when your change jar fills up, it's almost like getting free money. I've added to my investment account, and brought myself closer to my ultimate wealth goal, all for extremely little effort or sacrifice. Saving change is almost like a free throw in basketball. Why pass it up?!

When you are ready to deposit coins into your bank account, please take the time to put them in rolls if your bank requires it: please, please do not use a service like Coinstar that charges you as much as 10% to count and roll them for you! If you do, you're putting yourself

10% in the hole before you've even started investing. Some banks have coin counting machines in the lobby or in the teller area you can use for free. But if not, take the time to do it yourself. I want you to be posting very positive investment returns, not starting off with a 10% loss!

War Chest

Now we've reached the most difficult concept I want to impart to you when it comes to...I have to go back to that word again...saving.

Many, many books on personal finance will tell you it's extremely important to have 6 months of expenses saved and in the bank for emergencies and other unfortunate life developments than can occur. Some books tell you that you should have 6 months of your **salary** socked away for such emergencies (losing your job, health problems, a meteor landing on your car/house/head, etc.) It's a great idea, and I highly recommend it! But many of these same books tell you to build this fund and put it aside *before you do anything else* – that part I do not necessarily recommend.

So how many people do I know that have actually done this? I spent over 20 years in the financial industry, and of all the clients and colleagues I got to know over that time, if I count up all the people I have come across who have accomplished it, putting them all on a spreadsheet to make the job of counting easier, I can say quite confidently that the number in question is, exactly: 1. I do know someone who has at least 6 months of salary sitting in a bank account, waiting for an emergency. Of course, as far as I know, he makes several hundred thousand dollars a year, so...he doesn't count! I don't have that much money stashed away, and apart from the person I just mentioned, I don't know anyone else who does either.

Seriously though, it is a great idea, and over time...notice how I say OVER TIME...you should definitely do it. But it's certainly not where I would start. If you focus on socking away 6 months of you pay right off the bat, you're going to lose your perspective on **building wealth** and financial health; you'll get bogged down in a tedious exercise that is boring, depressing, and eventually won't even get done. So here's a better way to approach this:

Notice how I called this section War Chest. That's what I call my emergency fund (actually a friend came up with this name – that's one reason he was mentioned in the "Dedications"!). If it becomes time to go to war financially against some evil bill or expense that tries to invade my personal wealth, that's what I will turn to to fight it off. Though personally I'd rather not have go to *war* against an unforeseen bill, and I'd prefer to avoid even a minor skirmish. But having a War Chest will help you win such battles. I am building up a War Chest, and so you should you.

First, I'd have a little bit of a cushion in my bank account, as I talked about at the beginning of this chapter. Then, I'd wait until I could put together even a slightly-well diversified investment account, with at least, say, $5-10,000. Only then would I start to build the War Chest.

One way you could start to put money into your War Chest is create a line for it in your budget, if your finances will allow for it. Another is to set a benchmark for your investment account, say 5%, and any return you make in any given year above that benchmark, you take ½ of the additional profit out of your investment account and put it into the War Chest. That way you're using profits to build it up rather than sacrificing part of your hard-earned salary.

So where should your War Chest be kept? I suggest that you invest it too, but completely separate from your regular investment account. In fact, if you can find a money market account that pays over 1% per year in interest, that might be good enough for the War Chest. You want to manage the War Chest very conservatively, because you want the money to be available for emergencies at a moment's notice – you don't want to have to wait for investment prices or the market to rebound.

So now you should be on your way to building your wealth, and fulfilling some of the dreams you wrote down in the Planning chapter!

Debt – It doesn't have to be a 4-letter word!

Debt: the mention of the word can send chills up and down some people's spine!

What exactly is debt? It may sound like a stupid question, but there are different types of debt, and it's a good idea to know as much about them as possible: not only to keep yourself out of debt trouble, but also to use debt to your maximum benefit.

Debt, of course, is something that you owe to somebody else. Some people can't stand the thought of owing anything to anybody, so they avoid debt of all kinds at all costs. And if you can live your life without ever needing to go into debt (i.e. you are extremely wealthy or live a frugal lifestyle), then more power to you.

I titled this section the way I did because, even though there are 4 letters in the word, it's not always the evil concept people think it is. It's not a curse word, though it certainly can be a curse if you don't use it properly! Actually, there is such a thing as good debt, just as there is bad debt. More on that in a minute.

Since this book is geared toward U.S. college-aged people, I'm assuming you're probably living in the USA if you're reading this (or maybe you plan to move to the USA to pursue your university studies). If that's the case, I have news for you that might be viewed as bad, but doesn't have to be bad at all: chances are very, very high, upwards of 99%, that if you are not currently in some form of debt, you will be at some point in your life.

I'm sorry if that revelation frightened you! Actually, you probably knew that already. You will almost certainly have a car at some point in your life, and will eventually want to buy a condo or a house. While some people are able to pay cash for these items, most of us are not; we instead take out a loan (also known as a mortgage when it comes to real estate).

So, if you're afraid of debt, does this mean that you shouldn't buy a car until you can pay cash for it? Well, maybe, but my hope is to not make you afraid of debt, but rather to have you learn to use it wisely. For one thing, how many people can wait until they have enough cash to pay for the full price of a car?

This is why I say there is Good Debt and Bad Debt: debt **can**, when used properly, enable you to buy something you otherwise couldn't without harming your current lifestyle. In fact, there are times when it is beneficial to take on debt. Let me explain the difference between good and bad debt using a few examples.

Good debt

Here are examples of debt I would consider good debt. Before I show you the list, I will say again: these types of debt are good *only when used properly*! Good debt can be abused and turn into very bad debt. So, with that understanding, here are the types of debt I consider potentially "good":

- A car loan
- A mortgage on the place you will be living
- Student Loans

Here's why:

- <u>Car Loan</u>: if you do not live within walking/bicycling distance to work, and you don't live in a city that has a good public transportation network (I've just described at least

> *If you think nobody cares if you're alive, try missing a couple of car payments – Earl Wilson*

95% of Americans), you will need a car. Very few people have enough cash to pay the entire purchase price of a car. Taking a car loan will enable you to earn money you otherwise wouldn't if you were not able to physically get to the job location.

- o When good debt goes bad: you decide that your $35,000 annual salary will enable you to buy a $150,000 Maserati GranTurismo. If you take out a loan for which you have little if any hope of affording the payments, you have turned good debt into bad debt. Buy a car you can afford. Then your car loan is good debt.

- Mortgage: You need a place to live. Buying a house, or even a condo, can be a very good investment. It gives you shelter, and there is often a good possibility you can sell it in the future for more than you paid for it. Taking out a loan (mortgage) in this case is an example of good debt.

  - o But...just like in the car loan example, if you buy a home for which you cannot afford the payments, you are not using debt wisely, and the "bad" side to this type of debt will rear its ugly head. This is one thing that led to the housing bubble and subsequent crash of 2007-2008. People bought houses they couldn't afford, thinking housing prices *always* go up. They don't, and they didn't, and many people were left without a home.

- Student Loans: hopefully you will never need to take out a student loan to pay for your education. But if you do, you can think of it as an investment in your future. The repayment terms are favorable, and this can be a not-so-bad type of debt to incur.

  - o However, only take as much of a loan as you need, and start repaying it as soon as you can. Student loans can spiral out of control just like every other kind of debt can, so use them wisely.

Bad Debt

Even most of what I would consider "bad debt" can be ok if you use it sparingly and wisely. For example: credit cards. People can, and do every day, get in a lot of financial trouble by charging too much to credit cards. But if you use them to make occasional purchases that you currently don't have enough money in your bank account to cover, and then pay off the balance in a reasonable amount of time, credit card debt is not such bad debt. In fact, it can be a positive force in your life!

Most personal finance books will tell you that, if you use credit cards, you should pay off the entire balance every month. I'm not going to disagree with that – if you can do it, by all means do it. But if you have to make a purchase that improves the quality of your life and/or your happiness, and you can't pay the entire balance in full at the end of the month, don't beat yourself up about it. Pay it as soon as you can though. If you carry small balances on your credit card from one month to the next for a little while, it's not the end of the world, nor will it destroy your financial future. But try not to let balances linger for more than 4-6 months at the most.

First, a few examples of the wrong way to use credit cards, and then we'll take about how to turn them from bad debt to, well, not quite as bad debt (I'm not sure I would ever call them *good* debt).

I'm sure you've heard stories like this already, but I know plenty of people who started their credit card odyssey innocently enough by opening one account, with as little as a $200 or $300 credit limit. When you open that first account, and make your first charge, it feels like you're using free money! And, unfortunately, it can be addictive.

"A credit card is what you use when something costs too much and you want to pay more for it."

Suddenly you are able to spend more money than you ever could before: you can go more places, buy more things...even when that first statement comes in, it's not such a bad feeling: say you used all of your available credit in the first month, $300...all you have to pay right now is $25! So you bought $300 worth of stuff, and all you have to pay is $25??!! What could be better than that??

Well, eventually you will still have to pay the remaining $275, of course, with interest added in. But it doesn't feel that way at first. A lot of people look at this like, $25 per month is not too much to pay; so why not get another card, and all I will have to pay is $50 per month! I can handle that!

You can probably see where this is headed. When you look at credit cards as free money, and minimum monthly payments as all you really have to pay...as I said, it becomes addicting, and soon 2 accounts turns into 3, then 4, 5.....I've known people with as many as 15 open credit cards at a time. What happens in cases like this is that debt **snowballs**: more debt equals more interest owed on higher and higher balances, interests piles on top of interest making a larger and larger snowball hurtling down the hill, and eventually you can't even afford the monthly payments anymore. That's when serious trouble sets in.

If you've done this, or are headed in this direction, please don't feel bad about yourself, or panic. It's human nature to like to spend, and there is a rush you get when your buying power is increased, even when in the back of your mind you know you will have to pay everything back some day.

If you are in credit card trouble, you might want to skip ahead to the Managing Debt section of this chapter below. There's no magical way out, and I'll tell you right now, it probably won't be easy, but you **can** get out of debt and greatly improve the quality of your life. You can do it, all of you!

So now we'll talk about the right way to use credit cards, though I'll say right up front that credit cards really are best avoided as much as possible. Since establishing a good credit rating is important in the U.S., I'll say you probably should have one, but please, never more than 3-4 (1-2 is better).

The good news is that many credit cards give rewards to their cardholders; some of these rewards can be substantial. If you have the willpower to use them properly, you can get a lot of valuable benefits from having these accounts. Here are a few examples:

©Glasbergen
glasbergen.com

"The bank found suspicious activity on my credit card. It was being used responsibly to buy necessary things."

- **Cash back**: some credit cards give anywhere from 1-3% of your purchases using the card back to you in the form of cash, or they reduce your balance owed by this amount. This is like getting a 1-3% discount on everything you buy.

- **Store credit**: some retailers, or websites that sell a variety of goods and services, give you a percentage of your purchases back as store credit. In some cases, like Amazon, you can use your credit card to make purchases anywhere, and in return you receive 1-5% of the amount of those purchases to use at the issuing store or website. Amazon's card, for example, issues credit that can be used to buy anything you want on Amazon.com. Some gas stations have similar cards that allow you to get free or discounted gas.

- **Travel rewards**: Most airlines have credit cards available that allow you to earn frequent flier miles for every purchase you make with the card. These miles can be used toward free flights just the same as miles earned through travel can. In addition, some of the major hotel chains have credit cards that allow you to accrue points toward free hotel rooms.

So if you've decided you want to take advantage of some of these rewards, and you have the willpower to use credit wisely, here is what I suggest. Do you like to travel? Then open 1 credit card account with an airline; make it the airline that you are most likely to use (in other words, the one that has the most flights out of the airport nearest to you).

If you make frequent purchases on a particular website that has a credit card that offers rewards, open one with them too. And at the most, you could open 1 more account that offers cash back as a reward. Please do not open any more credit card accounts than these!

Of course, the best way to use these reward cards is to charge purchases *you were going to make with cash anyway* to these accounts, and pay off all the balances in full at the end of every month. You can also pay utility bills with them, as long as you send the money you were going to send to the utility company to the credit card instead. That way, you're not spending any more money than you otherwise would have, but you're also getting an extra bonus that you would not have otherwise received.

If you can't pay all of the balances in full at the end of the month, don't use any of the cards again until all balances are zero, and don't let it go more than 2-3 months before you make this happen. Make adjustments to your budget as needed.

I want to emphasize one more time a critical concept when it comes to using credit cards to accumulate rewards: use them only for purchases you were going to make anyway (preferably that were already in your budget)! Or use them to make an occasional small purchase for yourself as a treat. Don't use them to increase your general spending.

Keep your credit cards out of the realm of bad debt!

Personal loans and other bad debt

Banks out there are going to scream at me when I say personal lines of credit are a bad idea. There are times when they can be a great idea, especially if they can get you out of higher-interest-bearing debt, but as a young adult (which is who this book is geared towards, of course), there probably isn't any other need you would have for a line of credit. The good news is, at this point in your life, you're unlikely to get approved for one anyway! But I mention them because you've probably heard of them, and there may be a point in your life where it *might* make sense to have an open line of credit.

How it works is, a bank will assess your income and overall financial health, and if they decide you qualify, will tell you that you have $x available to you to take whenever you need, for whatever you need. It's pretty much like a credit card account: when you have a credit balance, you have to make a

> *A bank is a place that will lend you money if you can prove you don't need it –*
> *Bob Hope*

minimum monthly payment, and interest accrues on the amount of the balance you don't pay. Since lines of credit rarely give you rewards for using it (perhaps never – I'm not aware of one that does), they are, in a way, worse than credit cards. The appeal for people that qualify for them is that the amount of available credit is usually much higher than with most credit card accounts. But that means, of course, your ability to get into credit trouble with them is higher too.

Except for the use I will mention in the Managing Debt section below, at this point in your life I wouldn't even consider a personal line of credit. But as I said, you're unlikely to qualify for one anyway. And that's not such a bad thing!

Now here is the worst, absolute worst kind of debt you can take on: payday loans. Please, and I can't say please strongly enough, stay away from them at all costs!!! Yes, if you have a job they are easy to get, and you can walk out of the payday loan store with a handful of cash in just a few short minutes. But the interest you will pay is beyond astronomical!! At least with a credit card, in most cases when you pay the balance in full you are not charged interest. With payday loans interest is unavoidable, and it can be on the order of 500-1000% on an annual basis! Even the worst credit cards carry interest in the 30-40% range.

Absolutely no good can come from getting a payday loan, and you can easily wind up on the tragic treadmill of getting one loan just to pay off another. This is the equivalent of jet skiing toward financial disaster. Please, get payday loans out of your mind right now, and keep them out!!

Managing Debt

Getting into debt trouble is easy to do, and unfortunately it's a lot easier to get into trouble than get out of it. But don't worry, you can do it! Debt trouble is something that affects the overwhelmingly vast majority of Americans at some point in their life. Even as a young adult, it's easy to accrue debt problems. But if you make a commitment to solving those problems, you certainly can do it, and you'll be making your life much better in the process.

When I say "managing" debt, I mean getting to, and staying in, a desirable place in your life debt-wise. And only you can decide what that desirable place, or desirable state is. As I said earlier in the chapter, some people cannot stand being in debt of any kind. If you are one of these people, then managing debt should be easy: don't ever use any! Your desired state when it comes to debt is none. If this is you and you do have debt, read on; we'll get you back to zero!

If you don't think you have the willpower to use debt wisely, I suggest you become like the type of people I just described above: get to zero debt and stay there. Forget even credit card rewards. Tell yourself over and over if necessary, that debt is very bad for you, and you can't have **any** of it. No, it's not always as easy as that, just do your best to train your mind to think *zero debt*. Cut up your credit cards. Fight the urge to open new ones. All you can do is try!

For the rest of you, managing debt means getting to a place in which monthly credit payments are a very small portion of your budget (eventually going to $0 per month), and using credit cards to gain rewards as I explained a few pages back. With even just a bit of willpower, you can earn some valuable rewards and not harm your finances in the process. For those of you whole fall into this category, this is what managing debt is all about.

If you are in debt trouble, fear not: you can get yourself out. When people get into such debt problems that there is absolutely no other way out, many file Bankruptcy. Maybe you will have to do this at some point, though I seriously and sincerely hope not. Please try some of the methods I talk about for getting out of debt before you even contemplate the very drastic step of bankruptcy. It should be the absolute last resort.

Actually, the things I will tell you in the rest of this chapter are not revolutionary; they're not even new. You'll find the same types of approaches in most other personal finance books: where I'm going to try to add value to you is tell you what I think works best based on my many years of experience in the financial industry.

So let's assume you have too many open credit cards, all with maximum balances at the credit limit (we call this being "maxed out"). It's ok, many people are in a similar situation, and I too have been in credit difficulty in my life. But I got out, and so can you!

The first thing you might want to try is lowering the interest rate you are paying on your debt. Unfortunately this is very difficult, and does not have a high success rate (contrary to what some "experts" might tell you). There are several ways you can attempt this:

- You could call your credit card and other debt accounts (if you have any), and ask them to lower the interest rate they are charging you. Chances are, if you have a great deal of debt, some of your credit accounts carry high interest rates. Lowering the rate means you are paying less interest on a monthly basis, and can eliminate your debt more rapidly.

  ➢ Many personal finance books advocate doing this, and some say this is the very best way to get out of debt quickly. The reality is: it almost never works. You usually have as good of a chance of going to your local bank and expecting to be given free money.

     It's worth a try though; the only thing this costs you is a little bit of time. But be prepared to be rejected. Many years ago, I tried it with no success. Recently I had a friend who tried this, and was also quickly rejected. So he asked the person at the credit card company if they would rather give him a small break on his interest rate and get paid everything he owes them, or risk getting nothing back if he filed bankruptcy. They replied they would rather take their chances on losing all the money he owed them. This is the attitude of most credit card companies these days.

But try it anyway. If it works, it will indeed help you get out of debt sooner. But if you have a lot of debt, banks and other finance companies consider you a high risk for default; the last thing they will want to do is lower your interest rate, as they will not be getting compensated for the risk that you won't be able to pay them back (see the Investments section on Risk vs. Reward).

- You could also try what amounts to "refinancing" your debt at a lower interest rate by finding other credit cards to transfer your balances too. Some credit card companies will offer 0% or very low introductory interest rates for the first 12 months for example, after which the interest rate increases.

➢ This too is worth a try, but also does not have a high success rate if you are already in significant amounts of debt. The more open credit accounts you have, the fewer offers you will receive to open new accounts; and you will certainly stop receiving offers for lower interest rate accounts. But, if you can find a company willing to open a new credit account for you at a lower interest rate than one you currently have, by all means take it!

BUT!! **Only do this on one condition!** Promise me! If you are able to transfer a credit card balance from a card with a high interest rate to one with a lower rate, you MUST close the other card immediately!! If you keep both accounts open, you are not improving your situation, you are magnifying your problems big time!

If keeping the old account open and using the credit from it is even a slight temptation for you, DO NOT OPEN THE NEW ACCOUNT!!! Only refinance your credit card debt in this way if you are 100% certain you have the will power to close the higher rate accounts immediately.

So if/when you have tried lowering the interest rate on the debt you have to pay back, it's time to ramp up paying it back!

When faced with a list of large credit card balances, most financial professionals advocate one of two approaches: either pay off your highest interest-rate cards first, or start with the lowest balance card, and pay that one off first. Then the next highest, and the next highest after that, etc.. These are both very good approaches that have worked for many people. The thinking with the second method is that you'll get a psychological boost from paying off even 1 card, so go after the smallest one first to build up some momentum and give yourself a good feeling in the process. I agree this is a good method, but I'm going to propose something different to you.

I would prefer you attack your highest-interest accounts first, then move down the line as you go. The reason is that I want to ease the burden on your budget that credit card payments create as quickly as possible. So here is how I would start:

- Either on a piece of paper, or better yet using Excel, list all of your credit cards by name, amount you owe, and interest rate. You can find the interest rate you're being charged on your statement, either one that's being mailed to you every month, or probably more conveniently, online.

- Sort the accounts by interest rate, from highest to lowest. The one at the top of list is your first Elimination Target.

Credit Cards

Repay. Order	Name	Balance	Int. Rate
	Bank A	1200	17.2%
	Bank B	600	16.9%
	Bank C	2200	22.4%
	Bank D	1750	23.9%
	Store E	450	19.9%
	Store F	3400	14.5%

Then, hit Data, then Sort...sort by Int. Rate

Repay. Order	Name	Balance	Int. Rate
1	Bank D	1750	23.9%
2	Bank C	2200	22.4%
3	Store E	450	19.9%
4	Bank A	1200	17.2%
5	Bank B	600	16.9%
6	Store F	3400	14.5%

On your monthly budget, each of your open credit accounts should have their own line item. For all of your accounts except the Elimination Target, set your budget so that you are paying only the minimum payments each month.

Pretty standard stuff so far. But here's where I depart from a lot of other financial professionals: it's probably optimal from a finance standpoint to pay every penny you can to your Elimination Target account. So that means you would put no money into building wealth or adding to your investment account until **all** of your debt is completely paid off.

I suggest something different. I would adjust your budget so that, when all of your other bills and monthly credit card minimums are paid, you take 90% of what's left, and pay your Elimination Target card with it. Take the other 10% and put it in your wealth/investment account. Why? I believe it's important to build something on the positive side even when you are paying off debt. It's important to have something positive to show from your income.

You might even want to make it 80%/20%, or 75%/25%; whatever you feel most comfortable with. Whenever you get extra money – maybe you'll decide to take a second job, or you'll get a gift or find some way to make a little extra...whatever it is, whatever the source of extra income you might get from time to time: apply the same percentages to this money: use some to pay off the Elimination Target, and put the rest in your wealth/investment account.

In this way, you can continue to work towards a strong financial future by building on the positive side, and you can even get debt to snowball the other way! Here's what I mean by that: at some point you will pay off your Elimination Target account. The next credit card down on the list you made that was sorted by interest rate becomes your new Elimination Target. But not only will you have the amount you budgeted for the minimum payment to that card, you will also have the amount you had been paying to the previous Elimination Target card. So the 2nd card will be easier to pay off than the first, with each subsequent account you target for elimination easier and quicker to pay off than the last one. That's what I mean when I say you can have debt snowball in your favor. It snowballs when you're getting into it, but by using the above technique it can snowball on the positive side getting out of it.

Try it, it really works! I'm not saying it's going to be easy or quick, but it should get easier as you go. Think of the wonderful feeling you'll have when your debt is all gone! And then it's full steam ahead in building you wealth, and building the kind of lifestyle you want and deserve!

I'll end this section by telling you a story for those of you who are in a lot of debt and feel like you will never get out. It's a story about my father, who was one of the key inspirations for me to start writing. I consider my father to be the greatest man I ever knew, and he was living proof of how people could change and improve their life. At one point, he was in very bad credit trouble. He seemed to be drowning in debt, and it wasn't doing great things for his family's lifestyle.

But one day, something inside him said that's it, no more. He was determined not only to get out of debt, but to start to provide a better life for us and even build a strong retirement.

I wish I knew exactly how he did it. He had a very good job with an above-average income, but we were never by any means rich, or even close to it. He did work some pretty long hours for a while, and even took on an occasional side job as a locksmith, which he taught himself how to do. We lived a bit frugally for a while, but not that bad, and in a few years, the debt melted away.

Then he started putting money into retirement and investment accounts, much in the way I've suggested throughout this book, and it's amazing how things changed. We even started going on family vacations to nice places every year: Hawaii, California, Florida...people assumed that since we did a fair amount of travelling, we had a lot more money than we really did. Our improved lifestyle was due to a few key factors that my father brought into our lives:

- Getting rid of debt
- Finding a good balance between living a pleasant lifestyle today while also saving for the future
- Being moderately smart with money (again, finding a good balance between spending and saving).

And that was it! Nothing magical, nothing revolutionary. Just common sense. Finding the right mix between living for today and planning a better tomorrow. That's one of the many things I learned from my father, and that's what I want to pass along to you, my readers.

Retirement

OK, I get it, you're young, you have your whole life ahead of you...who wants to be thinking about retirement at your age?? I'm not suggesting you spend much time thinking about it, but you can certainly plan for it without dwelling on it.

> Retirement is wonderful. It's doing nothing without worrying about getting caught at it. – Gene Perret

Even so, I'm going to keep this chapter short, because in building current wealth you're already setting up a better retirement for yourself. You don't need to plan out every detail of your life 40-50 years from now, though its important you do the things I've recommended in the Planning chapter of this book. That's probably just as much thinking as you need to do about it at this point.

There are two things I would like to suggest, that are really part of the Investing section of the book that comes next. These are things you can do now, most likely, or if not now then soon, that will tremendously help build your retirement funds without the word "retirement" even coming into your head. And here they are, in order of importance:

401(k) Plan

If you have a job, you almost certainly know what a 401(k) plan is. But for those that don't, it is a type of retirement (oops, I did use that word after all, sorry!) savings plan that allows money to grow tax-free until you are older and eligible to start removing it. If you work for the government, or a government-owned entity such as a State university, this plan will be known as a 403(b), but it's the same thing.

How it works is, you contribute money into your account from your paycheck, before any taxes are removed. This lowers the amount of tax you pay, because your taxable income is lowered by the amount you contribute to your 401(k) every year. It also lowers the amount you actually receive from your employer (your take-home pay).

Most companies will even match the contributions you make to your plan, up to a certain point. We have a term for this in the world of Finance: free money!! For example, say the company you work for has a policy that says they will match your 401(k) contribution 100% up to 3% of your salary, and an additional 50% on the next 3%. Now let's say you are making $50,000 per year. Here is what will go into your 401(k) account over the course of the year:

- 3% of 50,000 is $1,500. So, $1,500 is removed from your paycheck during the year, and put into your 401(k) account. The company matches it, which means they put $1,500 into your account as well. Total from this phase: $3,000 going into your 401(k) account annually.

- Your company will match 50% of your contribution on the next 3% of your salary. So, if you take advantage of this, another 3% comes out of your pay ($1,500), and the company matches 50% of this ($750). Another $2,250 goes into your account.

- Total annual addition to your 401(k): $3,000 + $2,250 = $5,250. Total amount **you** have contributed to the account: $3,000. **Free money** you received: $2,250! And you can get this every year!

Over time, this can really add up. And the investments build up tax-free, until it's time to (yes, here it comes) retire. Since you did not yet pay tax on the amount you contributed, you will have to pay tax on money as you remove it from the plan. But this is a very, very good thing to participate in, believe me!

My recommendation is that you contribute as much as your plan and current government-set limits allow you too. However, I don't suggest you put yourself is a worse current financial situation to do it. Contribute as much as your budget will allow, because contributions lower your take-home pay. At a minimum, try your best to be able to take advantage of all the matches your employer will provide. So in the above example, I highly suggest contributing a minimum of 6% of your pay to your 401(k).

In the next section, I'll show you how to invest and allocate your 401(k) plan, but the message for now is: participate in it to the maximum you reasonably can.

Individual Retirement Account (IRA)

The acronym IRA means different things in different countries, but in the USA it stands for Individual Retirement Account. This works very much like your 401(k), but it is something you do yourself, rather than through the company you work for.

This type of plan is also funded with money before taxes are removed (pre-tax earnings), and also grows tax-free until taken out of the account. To get this type of plan started, contact any bank or investment company: my suggestion is to use an online brokerage firm (see the Investments chapter for more information).

You're not allowed to put as much as you want into this type of plan (there are also limits to how much you can put into an 401(k)), and the maximum has varied over time. In 2018 for example, you were allowed to put a maximum of $5,500 into an IRA. It might not sound like much, but this too can build tremendously over the course of a few decades.

What I've described above is a Traditional IRA; there is a variant known as a Roth IRA, which works a little differently, and is an outstanding idea for many people. If you're interested in learning more about Roth IRAs, and I highly suggest you do, please see the Building Lifetime Wealth website. I'll talk about them in detail and give you a few insights into them there.

So, should you contribute the maximum $5,500 to an IRA every year? If you're able to do it, absolutely, yes! But if you're in college, or recently graduated, or in the 18-25 age bracket, it might be a bit difficult to put money into both a 401(k) and IRA. In fact, not very many people in this age range can. It's ok! I suggest building up your 401(k) contribution to the point where you are taking full advantage of your employer's match first. Then, when and as your budget allows, you can start to think about opening an IRA.

One last word on saving for retirement. Yes, it's very important, and you will greatly thank yourself throughout your life for doing it, but one of the key themes of this book is to try to find a **balance** of living now and saving for later. I don't recommend making your life today a hardship, a tedious depressing exercise in which you save every penny you can for the future at the cost of having an unhappy life now. But I also recommend you don't spend every penny as it comes in, throwing caution and your future to the wind. There is a definite balancing point between the two. Unfortunately I can't tell you where that balance is, but I recommend you do your best to find it. Enjoy life, see the world, spend quality time with family and friends. But also do you best to build your wealth now and for the rest of your life.

You can be young without money, but you can't be old without it –
Tennessee Williams

SECTION IV – GROW

WATCHING A TENNIS MATCH

WATCHING THE STOCK MARKET

Investing

Like every chapter and section of this book, this part was written such that you can move around, and skip the areas that you already know about. I will start with very basic definitions of investments and investing terms, and get more advanced as the chapter progresses.

So you're getting your financial life on solid ground, and now you want to watch your money grow – good choice! Having some money in a bank account is nice (a great idea, actually), but it won't grow much. In fact, in *real* terms it won't grow at all, maybe worse (see the discussion about Inflation in Section I above).

We already talked a little bit about investing in the section on building a WarChest (see Section III). So when it comes to starting an investment account, or making investments in general, we'll assume you're going to be using money over and above what you think you will need to spend or put in a savings account.

First though, an explanation of the investment universe: what it is, what kinds of things you can invest in, and how it works. Then we'll talk about how to make it work for you!

Basic investment concepts

First, what is investing? Investing is using or spending a resource with the expectation of having more of something at some point in the future. Is that vague enough for you? Sorry! But that's a pretty accurate *broad* definition.

Essentially, investing is spending or using something **now** to put yourself in a better position in the **future**. There are number of things you can invest, not just money. You can invest time in a project in the hopes that the results will benefit you at some point, and be of more value to you *then* than your time is to you *now*. By reading this book you're investing your time, hoping to create a better financial future for yourself (I sincerely hope this investment pays off!). You can invest your energy, emotions...you can invest anything that is of value, hoping for a better future outcome.

But this book is about money, so we'll only talk about investing money. I already gave you a broad definition of investing, but I like the definition of investments when it comes to money that Investopedia uses, so here it is: an investment is a monetary asset purchased with the idea that the asset will provide income in the future or will be sold at a higher price for a profit (Source: Investopedia: https://www.investopedia.com/terms/i/investment.asp#ixzz4zZRBVpIL)

Investing vs Speculating

Here is where the definition of investing that many industry professionals use makes the topic a bit fuzzy. Investopedia's definition is quite correct, but it's also important to make a distinction between *investing* and *speculating*, or gambling. Investment professionals will tell you (correctly) that investing and speculating are two distinct entities, even though the broad definition of investing could encompass each.

Unfortunately there is no standard agreement on what exactly the distinction is between investing and speculating. Some professionals think it is **primarily** based on the amount/level of <u>risk</u> involved; I however, do not. Risk is part of the equation, as we'll see in a minute, but it goes deeper than that.

Besides the level of risk involved, here is the first of three additional things I believe separates an investment from a speculation:

- An **investment** is based on something <u>definable</u>, some quality within what is being invested in that you can <u>analyze</u> and <u>quantify</u>. To qualify as an investment, there has to be something *real for you to look at* to figure out how much whatever you want to invest in is worth to you now and potentially in the future.
- A **speculation** is a <u>bet</u>; a guess. It is something that has little or no objective data to analyze, the price of which is driven by emotion or luck rather than research.

There's a little more to it than that though. For example, a person might argue that, using the above criteria, betting on horses could be considered an investment. After all, you can analyze the horses' past performances, see which horse has run the fastest and won the most races. So should you take your investment

> *There are two time's in a man's life when he should not speculate: when he can't afford it, and when he can – Mark Twain*

money to the track? Please don't! Go for fun if that's what you want to do, but not to build up your investment account or your retirement fund!

There are two more elements that separate a speculation from an investment. Now we return to the concept of risk. First, to be able to realistically call something an investment, I believe there has to have a *low level of <u>random chance</u>* involved in its outcome. Second, the level of risk taken has to be rewarded with a similar, or at least close to similar, expectation of return on the money you put at risk (in other words, if you take a lot of risk, you should expect a high return on your money; if you take little risk, you can't expect as high of a return). Let me explain each of these concepts:

Let's look at 3 different events to illustrate the differences between investments and speculations: roulette, poker, and sports (just about any sport). First, roulette. Every spin of the wheel is a new outcome. Yes, there are people who chart the numbers that come up, looking for a pattern or a bias in the wheel (the casinos love these people by

the way). Most casinos even have an electronic scoreboard that shows the previous 10-20 numbers that have won (yes, they are encouraging people to play

systems, because they know they don't work and will lead to bigger bets and losses by those that use them).

But, unless there really is a flaw or bias in the wheel, which is very very unlikely, each spin is a completely new, random event, independent of all previous outcomes. So if "30" for example hasn't come up since last Tuesday, but "4" has just come up for the third time in a row, 30 is no more or less likely to come up than 4 on the next spin.

In Texas Holdem, each player is dealt 2 cards, and 5 cards are placed in the middle of the table as "community cards". These cards can be used by all players to build the best 5-card hand they can.

When I refer to the "flop", here is what I am talking about: after the players receive their 2 cards, the 5 community cards are placed on the table face down. After an initial round of betting, 3 of the community cards are turned face up. This is called the "flop". Another round of betting then takes place, as it does after the 4th and the 5th cards are revealed.

There is nothing to analyze, since all spins are random. Therefore, we can label roulette as a pure "speculation" (or gamble, of course), as are most other games in a casino.

> *There's a very easy way to return from a casino with a small fortune: go there with a large one – Jack Yelton*

Now let's have a look at poker, specifically the very popular Texas Holdem variant (different types of poker have different skill-vs.-luck ratios, but for the sake of this illustration when I refer to "Poker", I mean specifically Texas Holdem). Poker, unlike roulette, is a game you *can* win more often by being skilled rather than unskilled (sorry roulette fans, but there's no such thing as a skilled guesser). The poker industry is even trying to convince gaming regulators that poker is a game of skill rather than a game of chance, in an effort to get around gambling laws. Is it?

Well, yes and no. Before the hand begins, there is nothing to analyse; the cards that will be dealt are completely random. So, as in roulette, the initial outcome has no bearing on past outcomes: the chances of a player being dealt 2 Aces are 1 in 221 (or the "odds" are 220 to 1, in gambling-speak), and after the hand is over, the odds of being dealt 2 Aces again the next hand are still 220 to 1.

However, once the players' cards have been dealt, and again when the "flop" takes place, there is now plenty to analyze throughout the rest of the hand. Skilled players are able to calculate things such as the odds of having a winning hand given what has been dealt, the odds of drawing certain cards that will improve their hand, the expected % return on different levels of bets, etc.. While there is still a significant amount of random luck involved in the final outcome of the hand, at least poker has an element of skill and objective analysis to it. So does that make playing poker more like an "investment"? Let's look at our final activity before making that determination.

Now on to the world of sports. Obviously there is an enormous amount of skill involved in playing sports (except for maybe the Cleveland Browns). And yes, there is also an element of luck to all sports: a ball can bounce the wrong way or take an unfortunate rebound off a goal post, a player can accidentally trip and fall, a gust of wind can affect a throw or kick...any number of random things can and do happen in sports all the time.

But there's a reason that Tiger Woods has won so many golf tournaments, and Serena Williams so many tennis tournaments...there a reason Tom Brady's teams have won so consistently over the years, or why Lionel Messi scores so many goals...it's because skill plays a much, much bigger role in sports *over time* than does random luck. So in comparing various events to investments and speculations, sports comes closest to filling the role of an "investment": more skill than luck is involved. And poker? There's one more point I want to make before we can put a label on poker.

I consider myself a good, but not great, poker player. My skill level is absolutely nowhere remotely near that of players who win tons of money on the World Poker Tour, or in the World Series of Poker, for example. Yet I could potentially sit down and beat the best players in the world heads-up if enough cards fell in my favor. And so could you. Of course, the odds of that happening are small, probably extremely small, but they are not zero. The vast majority of the time, I would lose to such skilled players. But random chance could tip things in my favor enough that I could, on occasion, win.

However, there is **no chance** that I could ever beat players such as Jordan Speith or Tiger Woods in a round of golf, ever, no matter how much luck was on my side. The odds are not close to zero, they are *absolute zero*. Same as if I was stupid enough to step into the boxing ring with Floyd Mayweather. I wouldn't last 10 seconds before doctors would be retrieving random parts of my body to put back together from all corners of the ring! Again, absolutely zero chance luck could save me, or tilt things in my favor enough to even come close to winning.

That is how I see one of the differences between an investment and a speculation. In the example above, roulette is analogous to a pure "speculation", while sports takes on the role of being more of an "investment". Where does that leave poker? Unfortunately, it puts poker somewhere in between the realm of skill and chance, between "speculation" and "investment" (though in my opinion, due to the significant amount of random chance involved, poker is much closer to luck than skill). But many things you might consider "investing" in could fall into this murky in-between territory too.

So, as luck would have it (yes, I intended that pun...sorry!), there isn't always a clear defining line between an outcome driven more by luck or skill/analysis, or between an investment and a speculation. In fact, many things you will consider putting money into will fall somewhere on the investment/speculation spectrum without being purely one or the other. But that's ok, because as I'll say many more times in this book and on the website, investing is part art, part science. There are elements of each in choosing investments, creating portfolios, setting an asset allocation (and it's not necessarily a bad thing, trust me!). More on all of these topics shortly.

There is one more element needed for something to be called an investment, as I mentioned a few pages ago: you should expect a level of reward (return or profit on your investment) that at least matches the level of risk you take whenever you put your money at risk. The two don't have to be exact for something to be considered an investment, but they have to be at least close. If you are taking tons of risk for the chance to make very little profit, it's not an investment, it's a speculation (and a bad one at that!).

But if that same high-risk opportunities carries with it the chance for a high return, or lots of profit, then it *could* be called in investment (as long as the other 2 conditions I've talked about are also present). It might not be a great investment, but perhaps still an investment. Though I will say that something that has an **extremely** high level of risk, regardless of the potential reward, is likely not an investment.

To recap what separates investments from speculations (or bets), I believe all four of these must apply for something to be considered an "investment":

1. It must be something you can analyse with real, objective data.
2. It must be something that carries a relatively low level of random chance (luck).
3. It must offer a similar level of reward for the level of risk taken.
4. The level of risk should at least be somewhat reasonable.

Why is this important? It's very important, because it is critical to know the amount of risk you are taking with your money at all times, whether you are investing, speculating, or letting it sit idle. One of the most important principles in the world of finance, and critical to your success in personal finance, is that **risk and reward are linked together**. As I said a moment ago, the more risk you take, the higher reward in the form of the return on your investment (profit) you should expect. And vice versa.

It's also important to distinguish between investments and speculations so that you don't spend money on what you think is an investment, only for it to be a speculation in reality. We will talk much more throughout the book, and on the book's website, about how to allocate your money between different types of opportunities.

Defining Risk and Reward

We spent a lot of time talking about risk as it relates to investments vs speculation, because understanding risk is critical to understanding how to manage your money. It goes beyond the types of investments you might put into your brokerage account; it touches everything you will ever own.

So what exactly is risk? Put simply, it's the chance that you will lose something that you currently have. In the world of investments and personal finance, risk is the level of probability that you will lose money. Yes, it's that simple. But measuring it can be a lot more complicated.

Actually, when it comes to investing, risk isn't just that chance you will lose your money, it also involves how volatile your investments are, or how much their prices fluctuate. The most important thing of course is the prices at which you buy and sell an investment. But the fluctuation in their prices between these events can be important (more on that later), for investment and psychological reasons.

Some people cannot stand to see their account balance drop, even by a little bit, and even for a short time. Others hardly ever look at their balances, or prefer to keep an eye on the long-term and don't care about day-to-day fluctuations. Neither of these is right or wrong, it's just a matter of each individual's emotional makeup.

The degree to which you are willing and able to take on risk, either in terms of how much you gain or lose on an investment or its daily price fluctuations, is called your "risk tolerance". People who aren't willing to incur much risk are said to be "risk averse". Again, your risk tolerance level isn't something that's good or bad; it's something that is driven by emotion, personal preference, and your ultimate financial goals.

There are several ways to measure risk, and we'll talk more about them later in this section (as well as on the book's website), but the one I'll introduce first is Standard Deviation.

Now I can already see the eyelids starting to drop for those of you who are not mathematically inclined or a fan of statistics, so I won't go too deeply into this. I certainly don't have to tell you how to calculate it, because for one thing it isn't necessary: there are dozens, perhaps hundreds, of websites out there that will tell you, for free, what the standard deviation is of almost any investment you could buy. A good one, and one we'll talk about throughout this book, is Morningstar.com. But first, let's wrap up our discussion on risk, and get to something a lot more enjoyable: reward!

"I see your investments going up, but it's not clear which ones or when."

So, standard deviation is one of the most important measures of risk, and you can use it without even knowing much about it. The higher the number, the higher the risk. This makes it easy to compare the riskiness of many different types of investments, though one of its best uses is in comparing investments of the *same type*. We'll see this is more detail when we talk about the various kinds of investments you might want to consider later in this chapter, but for now, just keep in mind that standard deviation is a good tool to use to determine how risky many different types of assets are.

Ok, I promised you something more enjoyable, and here it is: reward. Who doesn't like to be rewarded?! And if you're putting your money at risk, you're going to expect to be rewarded for it. As I said earlier in this section, risk and reward are inextricably tied together. So what kind of reward can you expect from investing your hard-earned money? More money, of course!

In the investment world, we refer to reward as "return". The return on an investment is how much extra money it "returns" back to you. There are two potential sources of return from an investment:

- The difference between what you bought and sold it for (also known as the Capital Gain).
- Any additional income you received while you own it (often simply called Income).

The return you earn from the first bullet point above is obvious and easy to calculate. The second point, income you receive while owning an investment, usually comes from two sources: if you own stocks, you may (or may not) receive dividends, and if you own bonds, you will usually (but not always) receive interest (also known as coupon) payments. Adding Capital Gains and Income together gives you your **total return** on an investment.

To really understand what your reward for purchasing an investment is/was, it's necessary to turn the dollar amount into a percentage. After all, a particular amount of dollars can mean very different things to different people. And it also means very little until you put it into the context of how much you spent on it.

What if you were to say you made $1000 on an investment. That might be a very nice amount of money to you (and me – I'll take it!), but not be as earth-shattering for say, Warren Buffett or Bill Gates. The other questions are: how much did you invest to get that $1000, and how much time did it take you? If you invested $100,000 to earn $1000, it's not as big a deal as if you only invested $1000 to get it! And did it take you a month, a year, or 20 years to earn your $1000? Less time is, of course, better.

So that's why we need to turn investment returns into percentages, and, to address the second question above, convert them into an *annualized return*. This gives us a way to compare investments and to judge how well we have done in investing our money (or in the case of mutual funds, how well some else has done investing our money).

To annualize your investment returns, it's going to require a bit of math. Fortunately, the first part is simple (the second part isn't too bad either, but I know some of you out there really don't care for math, so just bear with me – it will be worth it). Here's the formula:

Total Return / Total Amount Invested

Not bad, right? You take what you earned, and divide it by what you invested. Don't forget to add any dividends or interest you earned while you held the investment (that makes it a *Total* return). But what we have at this point is your total percentage return; we still need to get to the annualized return. So here comes the rest of the formula:

$$[(1 + \text{Total Percentage Return}) \wedge (1/t)] -1$$

In the above formula, t = the time you held the investment in years.

OK, I realize that's a bit more ugly. But with a calculator, or better yet Excel, it's not so bad. I'll run through an example:

Say you buy 100 shares of a stock at $20 per share. That's a $2000 investment. The stock pays a quarterly dividend of 25 cents per share (which equals $1 per share per year). 4 years after you bought the stock, you decide to sell it when it reaches $23.20 per share. What's your annualized return? Let's use a calculator; to see how to do it in Excel, please visit the book's website. Here goes:

1. Calculate your total return in terms of dollars:
   - You sold the stock at $23.20 after purchasing it for $20.00.
   - You made $3.20 per share on the stock ($23.20 - $20.00 = $3.20). Multiplied by 100 shares, that gives you a Capital Gain of $320.
     - You could also have calculated the Capital Gain by taking the amount you received when you sold the stock, which in this case was $2,320 ($23.20 per share x 100 shares), and subtracted the $2,000 you paid for it ($20.00 x 100 shares). This gives you $2,320 minus $2,000, or $320.
   - You also earned $1 per share per year you held the stock. That's $1 x 100 shares x 4 years = 1 x 100 x 4 = 400. You earned $400 in dividends while owning the stock.
   - $320 Capital Gain + $400 Dividends Earned = $720 Total Return on the investment.

2. Now turn the dollar return into a percentage return
   - $720 return / $2000 you paid for the stock = .36   You made a 36% total return on your investment.

3. Finally, convert this into an annualized return
   - Turn the 36% into a decimal: 0.36, and add 1: 1.36
   - Raise this to the 1/t power, in this case 1/4 since the stock was held for 4 years. So it's 1.36 ^ .25. If you have a calculator that has a y^x key, enter 1.36, hit y^x; enter .25, hit y^x again, and you get 1.0799.
   - Subtract 1 from 1.0799, which gives you .0799. Turn this into a percentage and you get 8%. Actually you get 7.99%, but rounding it up makes it an 8% annualized return on your stock investment. Not bad.

Those of you who are mathematically inclined probably found this pretty easy. But before moving on, I'll run through a slightly more complicated example for the rest of you who are not math gurus, so that hopefully this process is a bit easier to understand.

So let's take the above example, but instead of buying 100 shares of the stock all at once, let's say you only initially bought 50 shares. Two years later, the price of the stock dropped to $18 per share, so you bought another 50 shares at this price. Another two years after that, you sold all 100 shares at $23.20 just as in the previous example. Here's how to get the annualized return in this case:

1. Total Dollar Return:
   - You still sold 100 shares at $23.20 per share, to receive $2,320 when you sold the stock.
   - Your purchase amount has dropped to $1,900. This is because you only bought 50 shares at $20.00 per share ($1,000), and another 50 shares when the price dropped to $18.00 per share ($900). Adding these two purchases together gives you a total amount invested of $1,900.
   - Your Capital Gain is now $420 ($2,320 sales proceeds minus $1,900 you invested in the stock).
   - The amount you received in dividends has also changed. For the first two years, you were paid $100 in dividends (50 shares x $1 per year x 2 years = $100). For the final two years, you received $200 in dividends (100 shares x $1 per year x 2 years = $200). $100 + $200 = $300 total received in dividends.
   - Your total dollar return is $720 ($420 Capital gain + $300 in dividend income).

2. Total Percentage Return:
   - Total Dollar Return of $720 divided by total amount invested of $1,900 = .3789, for a total percentage return of 37.89%

3. Annualized Return:

- .3789 + 1 = 1.3789. This number needs to be raised to the 1/t, or 1/4 power just as in the previous example (since it was also held for 4 years), which equals 1.0836
- Subtracting 1, and converting to a percentage gives you a return of 8.36%.

This same procedure can be used to calculate the return of any investments of any type, including entire portfolios (though it gets more complicated when looking at portfolios of assets that have differing purchase and sell times, but I will cover that in future books). It's a matter of adding up purchase amounts, dividend or interest income received while holding the investment, calculating Capital Gains, and plugging the numbers into the above formula. And now you know how to calculate return, which is your reward for purchasing an investment!

Wrapping up Risk and Reward

Now that we have defined risk and reward (return), as well as shown you how to look at them both in terms of numbers and percentages, here are a few key points about the relationship between the two:

- If you decide to increase the amount of risk you take, you should expect to have the chance to earn at least a correspondingly higher return.

- If you don't take much risk, you can't expect, over the long-term, to earn as high of a return as riskier investments would provide.

- Through building a diversified portfolio of investments, you can lower your overall level of risk without significantly lowering your return expectations (see Diversification and Diversification Part II below)

Yes, the first two points above are saying the same thing, but they are different ways of looking at the **risk/reward tradeoff**, and far too many investors don't seem to be able to grasp this concept. Study it, learn it, embrace it. It's not difficult, but failing to understand and remember this basic principle will almost certainly lead to not making nearly as much money on your investments as you should (or even lose where you should be winning). You don't have to memorize it – we will be talking a lot about it throughout most of the rest of the book. It's that important.

Before taking a look at how to build your investment portfolio, and how you can use the power of diversification to improve your own risk/reward expectations, let's have a look at the various types of investments you might want to consider purchasing (or not – you'll understand as you go through each section) at some point in the future.

Stock

When you buy stock, you purchase "shares" of the company, because what you are really buying is a *share* in the ownership of that company. If you buy 100 shares of Amazon or even 1 share, you own part of Amazon! If you buy either of those two amounts, don't expect Amazon's CEO Jeff Bezos to pick up the phone when you call. But you are still an official, and legal, part-owner of Amazon.

So why won't Mr Bezos want to speak to you if you call? Because even if you buy 10,000 shares, which would cost a considerable amount of money (tens of millions of dollars), you would still only own something like only 0.002% of the company. But most people that buy Amazon's stock aren't doing it to get on Mr Bezos' speed dial!

There are really two main reasons why you might want to buy stock. I've already mentioned the first: because you're hoping to get more money out of the investment than you put into it. Does anyone ever hope to get *less* money from something they invest in? Very unlikely. Profit is really the main motivation for the vast majority of people who buy stocks (or any other type of investment).

The other reason people might buy stock in a company goes back to the first thing I talked about in this section: they want to have a piece of the ownership of the company. And even that can be broken down into two different purposes: 1) to have influence in the management of the company (or even to gain control of it), or 2) just to satisfy a wish to say you are part owner of the company.

Before talking about the first purpose above, I'd like to make a few comments on why anyone would do the second. Actually, I've done it. Many years ago I bought shares of the Tribune Co. because they owned the Chicago Cubs, and I was a Cubs fan at the time. I didn't really care if I made money on the investment, I just wanted to be able to tell people I was part owner of the Cubs! Of course that, along with $6, would get me a hot dog at Wrigley Field! Other than that, it meant nothing, except to me. My ownership stake was on the order of 0.0000001% of the company, so I wasn't exactly expecting team management to call me for advice before making trades.

People buying stock in companies that own sports teams that they like is not too uncommon. But an extreme example is the Green Bay Packers. There are Packers' fans all over the world, and they are particularly rabid about their team, for good reason: it's one of the most storied and successful sports teams in North America. And you can buy stock in the team (not just a parent company that owns the team)!

But before you empty out the piggy bank (or investment jar, or even investment account!) to buy a few shares, there are a few things you

 should know, which are about as favorable as a blocked punt: unlike almost every other stock you can buy, you can't sell Packers stock except back to the team: at a fraction of the $250 per share you have to pay for it! It pays no dividends (not unusual though), and gives you no real ownership stake in the team (highly unusual). You don't even get a discount on tickets. But you do get one of those stylish cheese-shaped cheesehead hats that Packers fans like to wear…for a fee. All you *really* get is a piece of paper and the knowledge that you essentially donated money to the team.

If you buy stock in a company just because you want to own a piece of it, and you really don't care whether you make money on it….I won't tell you not to do it, but just be aware it's not exactly a winning *investment* strategy. As I said, I've done it myself. But please, don't put money *you need to reach your ultimate financial goals* into stock like this – use your play money instead. I'll talk more about investing money vs "play" money shortly.

Another point I'd like to make before we dive deeper into the characteristics of stocks is that, for the rest of the stock discussion below, I'll be talking about **common stock**. There is another type called *preferred stock*, but this is less common (you can decide for yourself whether I intended that pun!), and personally I don't think it has much use or benefit for most investors. I'll discuss preferred stock on the book's website if you are interested in learning more about it, but I won't really talk much more about it in this book.

So what do you get if you buy shares of a stock? Hopefully more than just a cheesehead hat! I've already talked about a few of these, but

> *Do you have any idea how cheap stocks are? Wall Street is now being called Walmart Street – Jay Leno*

here is a basic list of stockholder rights as well as things you might be able to get:

Rights:
- A piece of the ownership of the company (also known as an equity stake).

- The right to vote on important company issues, such as mergers and the Board of Directors (or to have someone vote your shares for you).

- The right to share in whatever is leftover in the company's assets should a liquidation take place (such as following a bankruptcy filing) after bondholders and just about everyone the company owes money to have received their share.

Well, yes, you get these rights. But unless it's a very small company, or you can afford to buy a huge amount of the company's shares, the first two rights aren't ever going to do you much good. The third point above is something you will likely never see. If you own stock in a company that goes bankrupt, here's how to calculate how much you are likely to receive: get out a calculator, and hit the 0 button. Sorry, but that's usually what's left over for stockholders after a bankruptcy filing.

OK, so the rights are not so good. Then why buy stock? It all comes back to the first reason I mentioned a few paragraphs back: to get more money out of it that what you put into it. As we saw in the examples of how to calculate the annualized return of an investment, this can come from two sources: rising prices (also called price appreciation, which can lead to capital gains when you sell the stock), and dividends.

First, a few words about dividends. Not all companies pay them, but when a company has more cash than it needs, or wants to return money to shareholders for other reasons (perhaps to make its stock more attractive), it may give some of that money back to its shareholders in the form of a dividend.

Most companies in the U.S. that pay dividends do so quarterly (every 3 months, or 4 times per year). Occasionally a company will declare a special, one-time dividend, but this is rare. A company is under no obligation to ever pay a dividend (a lot of technology companies, and many smaller, newer companies do not), and those that do pay them can stop at any time. So if you buy stock you don't have a **right** to receive a dividend. They are completely at each company's discretion.

Dividends can be great, but here's a classic mistake investors often make: focusing too much on the money you receive in the form of dividends, and not on the whole picture, which includes the money you make or lose when you sell the stock. If you buy a stock because its dividends are yielding 8% (more on that in a moment), but you sell the stock for 5% less than what you bought it for, you didn't really earn 8%.

Another common mistake that less-experienced investors often make is failing to account for the drop in the value and price of the stock after a dividend is paid. If a stock is worth (or trading on an exchange for) $10 per share, and pays a $1 dividend, it is now worth

"IT'S HIS ONLY FORM OF EXERCISE THESE DAYS -- CHASING YIELD."

(or trading at) $9 per share. The value, or price of a stock is always decreased by the amount of any dividend the underlying company pays. Dividends aren't free money! Many investors lose sight of that.

I mentioned dividend yield: this is simply the amount of dividends a company pays as a percentage of its stock price. This gives investors an idea of approximately what kind of percentage return they can expect to earn just on the dividend portion of their investment should they buy (or continue to hold) the stock.

But as I said, be careful of this statistic. A struggling company will often cut or eliminate their dividend as one of their first money-savings tactics. I've implied this already, but now I'll come out and say it: don't ever buy a stock just because of its dividend yield! There are two factors involved in how much money you'll make from any investment: income and capital gains. Pay attention to _both_!

A few pages back, I promised to talk about one of the possible reasons someone might want to buy stock in a company other than just to make capital gains or income: to gain control of the company. For most of us, this will never really come into play. Every see the move Pretty Woman? That's what Richard Gere's character did: buy enough shares of a company to gain control if it, and break it into pieces, making even greater profit selling the pieces. Michael Douglas's character in the classic movie Wall Street (Gordon Gecko) did something similar, though it didn't work out so well for him: he went to jail instead of riding off into the sunset with Julia Roberts! I just wanted to mention this as a possible reason for buying stock, even though it's one very, very few people ever will use.

Let's move on to other types of investments, since this is not a book on security analysis and selection; though I will talk in great detail about these subjects in future books and on the Building Lifetime Wealth website.

Bonds

With all due apologies to bond owners, fans, traders, aficionados, and bond salespersons, most people do not find bonds nearly as exciting as stocks. There's probably a reason a lot more movies have been made about the stock market and stock traders than bonds (I can't think of any). To continue with the movie theme, stocks are the high action thriller of the investment world, while bonds are more like a documentary on the plight of the spotted owl in northern Peru.

But if bonds are less exciting then stocks, they are certainly no less important to investors, the companies/governments that issue them, or the global economy. Without bonds, companies could not build factories; many things like bridges, hospitals and stadiums would probably never be built, and the economy of the world would come to screeching, grinding halt. Not bad for something that is usually considered the boring, ugly stepchild of the investment world.

What is a bond? At its basic level, it's really just a loan. Money is being loaned by the bond buyer to the bond issuer. When you buy a bond (assuming you don't but it from another investor), you are loaning money to the company or governmental entity that sold it to you, usually for a specified amount of interest, and for a specific amount of time. And if you do buy a bond from another investor (which is what usually happens when you trade in the standard investment markets), you're just assuming the loan and its terms from the original buyer.

How it works is: you buy the bond, and the issuer agrees to repay the money it borrowed at some date in the future, with interest. Exciting, yes? Ok, not really (told you). But it is pretty simple. So why is the bond world in reality so very complicated (incomprehensible to some)? Because there are a lot of quirks, twists, and additional features to the simple loan-with-interest concept that forms the heart of what a bond really is.

We won't go into all of those quirks and twists in this book, and believe me, even if you don't realize it, you're grateful! But we will talk about the important things you will need to know as a bond investor, and trust me on this, you will almost certainly want to be a bond investor in one form or another.

Let's look as some practical examples of how bonds work, which is the best way for you to gain the knowledge you need before investing in them. First, we will look at a typical corporate bond as they exist in the USA:

Company XYZ wants to raise money to fund some sort of project or purchase, and they decided to do it by selling bonds to investors. Let's say they need to raise $10 million, so they decide to issue 10,000 bonds at a price of $1000 each. They also decide that, in order to make the bonds more appealing to investors, they will offer 8% annual interest to the original buyers. The purchase price of the bonds will be returned to the buyers in 30 years, and in the meantime the buyers will receive $80 per bond per year in interest (8% of $1000).

Here are the key things to know about these bonds:

- The day 30 years from now that the $1000 purchase price will be returned to investors is called the Maturity Date. It can be said the bonds will mature in 30 years. Next year these bonds will mature in 29 years, the year after in 28 years, etc.

- The amount that will be returned to the buyer on the Maturity Date (in this case the $1000) is called the Par Value. A Par Value of $1000 is standard (but not required) in the U.S.. Bonds do not have to be sold at the amount of the Par Value (and very likely won't be on the secondary markets); they can initially be sold at whatever price the issuer wants, though they have to set a price that enough people will want to pay if they want to raise all the money they need! It's very typical for a bond to originally be sold in the primary market at its par value, as is the case in our example.

- It's standard (but again, not all bonds are set up this way) for bonds issued by corporations in the U.S. to make interest payments twice per year (semi-annually), once every six months. Since the bonds in our example will pay $80 in interest to the holders every year, each payment the holder receives will be $40. The $40 semi-annual payments are known as the Coupon Payments.
  - Why "Coupon Payment"? Because initially, back in the dark ages before computers, the Internet, and (gasp!) Instagram existed, the buyers of bonds would receive a certificate with actual coupons attached that they would have to mail (or present in person) to the company to receive their interest payment. Now of course everything is recorded and handled electronically, but for some reason the term Coupon Payment has survived. Crazy bond world!

- So let's say you decide to buy 10 of these bonds at $1000 each. $10,000 will be deducted from your investment account and be sent to Company XYZ, and 6 months from now (and every 6 months thereafter, unless you sell the bond) you will receive interest (coupon) payments of $400 ($40 times the 10 bonds you purchased). 30 years from now, your $10,000 purchase price (par value) will be returned to you.

What's that: you don't want to wait 30 years to get your money back? That's ok, most of the time you can sell your bonds to another investor in the Secondary market. But beware, there might not be anyone willing to pay you $1000 each for them. Then again, maybe the going price for these bonds is more than $1000! In that case, you'll get a little extra money above the coupon payments you've received and the par value of the bond.

Actually, bonds trade in investment markets just like stocks do. Prices go up and down, just as they do for stocks, though bond prices typically don't fluctuate nearly as much as stock prices. This means, just as for stocks, you have to be mindful of potential price movements and not just look at the expected yield from the interest payments.

So if bond prices fluctuate, how exactly do you know what kind of return to expect if you want to buy a bond? I'm glad you asked, because that gives me the chance to introduce you to two more exciting concepts from the world of bonds: Yield-to-Maturity, and the inverse relationship between bond prices and interest rates! And when I say exciting, I mean...well, not all *that* exciting. But they are very important (no joke).

So, to answer the first question above, you can know exactly what return to expect from a bond that you are considering purchasing today. It comes from something called

Primary vs Secondary Market transactions:

Transactions that take place in what is called the Primary Market happen directly between the investor and the company or governmental entity that issued the security (bond or stock).

Secondary Market transactions take place between investors only – the underlying company is not involved in any way. For most transactions, when you buy stocks or bonds in a brokerage account, you are really buying them from another investor, not from the company that issued them. The vast majority of investment transactions take place in the Secondary Market.

Yield-to-Maturity (also called YTM, which is what we'll call it from here on). This will tell you the exact return (also called yield) you will earn, if (see if you can figure this out from the name) you hold the bond *to maturity*. If not, if you plan to sell the bond before it matures, YTM is not necessarily as useful to you, but still important to know.

I could, at this point, spend some time telling you how to calculate YTM, but I think I'll be kind and save it for the book's website and future books (again, if you're not full of gratitude, you should be!). Also, there are only like a hundred or so websites you could instantly find the YTM for any bond trading in the market, so it's really not necessary to know how to calculate it unless you are a math fanatic or are taking one of my introductory finance classes (if this is you, I really will discuss calculating YTM on the Building Lifetime Wealth website).

If YTM it isn't always all that useful, why bother spending any time talking about it? For one thing, maybe you will buy a bond with the intention of keeping it until it matures. That would make YTM extremely useful. It can also help you compare the attractiveness of different bonds from a purchase perspective. And it helps illustrate the next concept I want to tell you about: the inverse relationship between prices and interest rates when it comes to bonds.

Did you ever play seesaw when you were a kid? Personally, it wasn't my favorite game on the playground, but the concept is simple enough: when one end goes up, the other end comes down. If one end goes up fast enough, the other end hits the ground pretty hard (which is one of the reasons I wasn't crazy about it)! Both ends can't go up at the same time, nor down at the same time: when one end of the seesaw moves in one direction, the other end *has* to move in the opposite direction. Maybe if I had known how much it could have taught me in the future about how bonds work, I'd have been a bigger fan of seesaw when I was a kid! Probably not.

So you get the point, I'm sure: when bond prices go up, YTM comes down, and visa versa. Why does this have to happen? Because, as I've already said a time or two in this book, investment returns have two components: Income and Capital Gains. The interest you receive when you hold a bond is the income portion of your reward; YTM takes into account the Capital Gains portion as well. A higher price means that the interest payments are a smaller percentage of that price: price up, interest *rate* down.

To see how this works, let's go back to the example about of Company XYZ's bonds. When they were issued, the bonds cost $1000 each and paid 8% interest per year. Now let's fast forward to one year later. Investors are so impressed with Company XYZ's operations and profits, and they like the big coupon payments so much, they're willing to pay more than $1000 to own the bonds. Let's say the bonds are currently trading at $1100. If you decide to buy one of these bonds now, you'll pay $1100, but when it matures, you'll still only get $1000. So you will have a Capital Loss of $100. The coupon payments will still be 8% of the par value for as long as you hold the bond, but that's 8% of $1000, not 8% of $1100. So the YTM comes down below 8% to adjust for the $100 you will lose on the bond at maturity based on the $1100 you paid to receive $1000.

Why would anyone do this? Because even though you lose $100 based on the price you paid for the bond, the coupon payments might more than make up for this. Let's say the bond we've been talking about has 5 years to go before it matures. Without going into how to calculate it (again, see the book's website if you want to learn how to do it), the YTM on this bond is still around 5.7%. That's not a bad return for a lot of bonds!

Before we wrap up our discussion about bonds, let's turn to the risk side of the risk/reward equation, since we've spent most of this section talking about returns. We've seen how to assess the reward potential of a bond (YTM), but how do we know how risky a bond is? There are two ways: you can dig through the company's financial statements, annual reports, quarterly reports, news stories, call investor relations, play golf with the CEO.....or, you can look at the bond's rating. Actually, if you *can* do the first method (maybe minus the golf), it's probably the best of the two. But who, apart from professional analysts, has time to do all that? So, you will probably want to use the far less perfect but far, far less time consuming second method: look at the rating.

Like many things in the bond world, I am convinced the rating system was designed to provide potential investors like you and me with the maximum level of confusion possible. To explain, we will only look at the systems used by the world's two largest bond rating agencies: Standard & Poor's (more commonly known as S&P), and Moody's.

Each agency assigns a letter rating to the bonds it covers; you might expect the letter A to be the highest rating. Well, almost. Actually, it's AAA. Ok, that's not so bad. The next level down is AA, and then A (actually for Moody's, the top 3 levels are Aaa, Aa, and A. I guess they just wanted to be a little different).

Moving below A, you would expect the pattern to continue, with the next level being BBB. Yes, except for Moody's, which decided to make their next level Baa. Either Mr. Moody was also a sheep rancher, or his printing press had a shortage of "B"s (and too many "a"s) Next we go down to BB (Ba in Moody-land), and then B for both. Then of course CCC/Caa, CC/Ca and C/C. Then DDD, right? Wrong. Just D, which stands for Default, which leads to.....bankruptcy court. If a bond is in Default, it means the issuer missed a coupon payment, and that almost always forces the company to file bankruptcy. Which is not a good thing for bond holders, though they usually will recover at least some of their investment (unlike stockholders, who almost always get nothing from a company in bankruptcy).

As if this wasn't exciting enough (and as clear as mud), the rating agencies also assign plusses and minuses (+ and -) to each level. So on the BBB level, for example, bonds could be rated BBB+, BBB, or BBB- in descending order of how attractive the bond is from a less-risk standpoint. Oh wait, that's just S&P; Moody's of course doesn't have a BBB tier, it uses Baa instead. And it also doesn't use +'s or −'s, it decided to go with 1, 2, and 3 instead. 1 is equivalent to S&P's "+", while 3 is the same as a "-". So a bond rated BBB- by S&P would receive a Moody's rating of Baa3. Who said bonds aren't any fun?!

Rather than memorizing the entire rating system (I think the people at Moody's invented theirs after a few people got overserved at the company holiday party), it's important to understand how it works at a basic level. The A levels are better than the B's, AAA is better than AA, etc. The key takeaway from the rating system should be that, as you move down the rating scale, the level of risk rises. So a AAA bond has less risk than a BBB bond for example.

And what should you expect from something that has higher risk? Higher reward, you're right! So should a BB bond have a higher YTM than a AA bond? Absolutely. Less risk (higher rating) = less reward (lower YTM). More risk (lower rating) = more reward (higher YTM).

One last thing about bond ratings, I promise! There are two main categories of bonds and their ratings when it comes to risk: Investment Grade, and Non-investment Grade. Investment Grade bonds are those rated BBB- and higher (Baa3 and higher by our friends at Moody's), which means that Non-investment Grade bonds start at BB+ (Moody's: Ba1) and go lower down the rating scale.

This is an important distinction, because many institutions and foundations are forbidden by their charters to hold Non-investment Grade bonds for risk management reasons. It's very possible you'll be asked to sit on an investment committee of one of these organizations at some point in your life (even if you are not much of an investment person), so that's one reason you should know the distinction between the two categories.

A more likely reason is that bond mutual funds are often distinguished by whether they invest in Investment Grade or Non-investment Grade bonds, and as you'll see in the next section, you will probably be a holder of a bond mutual fund or 2 (or several) throughout most of your investing life. So when it comes to bond risks, even if you don't memorize every paragraph above, knowing the basic principles could help you move from a good investor to a great investor!

The last thing I want to leave you with when it comes to bonds is the various types of bonds you might invest in (or more likely will buy mutual funds in). We've used the example above of a Corporate bond, and I won't go into nearly as much detail with the other types. I will just list them below with some of their key characteristics. More details and distinctions will be available on the Building Financial Wealth website.

Broad Bond Categories:

Government Bonds: These are bonds issued by the U.S. Government. They are also known as "Treasuries". Since they are backed by the "Full Faith and Credit of the U.S. Government", they are one of the safest investments you can make, and certainly carry the least risk of anything else available in the bond universe. The government issues Treasury Bills, Treasury Notes, and Treasury Bonds, though it's typical to call all of these simply "Treasuries" (the distinction between them can be found on the book's website). The U.S. Government has never defaulted (or failed to make interest payments/par value repayments) on a bond, which is one reason they are all rated AAA.

Since they carry the least risk, they generally offer the lowest yields amongst all bonds.

Corporate Bonds: We've already covered the details above, so suffice it to say these bonds usually carry more risk and therefore higher yields than Government bonds.

Municipal Bonds: Also known simply as "Muni Bonds or Munis", these are bonds issued by a state or local government. By U.S. law, the interest earned on the bonds are tax-free (though any Capital Gain you make on them is not). Therefore, their yields tend to be lower than on other types of bonds (I will discuss tax-equivalent yields in a future book). Even though they are issued by governmental entities, risk levels range from low to very high. Be sure to pay attention to ratings, interest (coupon) rates and tax-equivalent YTMs before investing in munis. Most ordinary investors tend not to purchase muni bonds.

Other bond definitions to know:

Agency Bonds: Issued by agencies of the U.S. government as well as quasi-governmental entities. These bonds range from attractive to best-avoided investments. Do plenty of research before buying individual Agency Bonds.

Mortgage-Backed Securities: These bonds are backed, or payment of interest and par-value contingent on, pools of mortgages, the payments from which are used to make payments to bondholders.

Inflation-Protected Securities: Worried about the effects of inflation on your investment? These bonds have the amount of their coupon payments and payouts at maturity adjusted to counter those effects. When inflation goes up, so does the coupon rate and maturity value.

Zero-Coupon Bonds: As the name would suggest, the coupon (interest) payments on these bonds are zero: they do not make interest payments. So where does the reward aspect come from? These bonds are sold below their par value, so your return is completely based on the difference between what you pay and the par value. Typically these bonds have a maturity of 1 year or less.

Premium Bonds: The word "Premium" usually denotes a higher quality product, or something that is better than just "standard"...except in this case. When it comes to bonds, "premium" just means that the bonds are selling above (or at a premium to) par value. So therefore the YTM is lower than the coupon rate.

Discount Bonds: These are bonds that are selling below (or at a discount to) par value. That means they will have a higher YTM than their coupon rate.

So now that we've reached the end of our discussion about bonds, I'm going to tell you something that I hope won't make you angry with me: you will probably never buy an individual bond. I have been investing for around 30 years, and I have never bought an individual bond in my life. So why spend so much time on the details of individual bonds? Because very, very few of you reading this book will *not* be a bond investor at some point, if not every point, for the rest of your life. And knowing how bonds work will make you a better investor. But you will most likely own **bond mutual funds**, which is what I recommend for the vast majority of investors.

If you become relatively wealthy at some point, and I sincerely hope you do, you might want to add individual bonds to your portfolio. Or you might hire a professional manager to choose individual bonds for you. But most people are better off sticking with mutual funds. Which, as luck would have it, is the topic of the next section!

Mutual Funds

Mutual Funds will almost certainly be one of the most important types of investments you will ever make. They are easier to buy, sell, manage and analyze than individual stocks or bonds for most non-professional investors.

Before launching into a discussion about how you can use mutual funds to greatly improve your financial life, let's define exactly what a mutual fund is. A mutual fund is an investment company (which is what they were originally known as) that takes money from a large number of investors, and builds diversified portfolios that those investors likely could not build for themselves. Having a large pool of money allows the manager to buy investments much more efficiently than most individuals (who have a lot less money) could do on their own.

Example? Want to buy all 500 stocks in the S&P 500 index? Do you have enough money to buy at least 1 share of 500 different stocks? No? Not many people do. But you could buy a mutual fund that would allow you to own a piece of all 500 of these companies for a relatively small amount of money.

That's part of the beauty of mutual funds: they are a tool (remember the discussion about tools?) that can allow you to invest in things you otherwise could not. This tool gets its name from the fact that it is a pool of money (otherwise known as a fund) that is managed for a group of people who have invested in common (or mutually), hence: mutual fund.

It's that simple! And they do simplify life for a great many people. Their simplicity makes them so useful as a tool. However, building a diversified portfolio of mutual funds, and knowing which funds to choose, requires a bit more knowledge (which fortunately you can get from this and future books!).

Wait a minute – didn't I just say mutual funds give investors diversification they couldn't get for themselves? So *more* diversification is needed? Yes. Even though most mutual funds are rather diversified investments, they themselves need to be diversified in your portfolio as well. One of the reasons is no one mutual fund by itself can create the type of portfolio of stocks, bonds, and other types of investments you will need to be properly diversified (some try, but I don't recommend them).

Style categories

Before actually building a portfolio of mutual funds, it's necessary to know how they are classified: you need to know what the materials are that you are using to build or make something before you actually make it, right? If you want to make a sweater and all you have on hand is a box of bricks, you might want to think twice before you start knitting. Actually I had a sweater once that looked like it was made from a box of bricks...but that story probably belongs in a different book!

In a little while, we'll be talking about the most important aspect of your portfolio, Asset Allocation, but we'll need to at least define what those assets are that you will be allocating before we get to that section, and so that I can help you understand the importance of style categories in the world of mutual funds.

Investments that you will want to consider buying, or for building any kind of an investment portfolio, fall into what are call Asset Classes. By separating these "assets" into "classes", it makes it easier to see how much risk you are likely to be taking on, and of course, how much of a reward you should expect.

We've already spent a lot of time talking about the two largest asset classes: stocks and bonds. The asset class that stocks fall into is often called Equities instead. Bonds are often called Fixed Income products, and are thus in the asset class called Fixed Income by most investment professionals. Many people consider Cash to be a separate asset class, but a lot of investment professionals instead include a portfolio's allocation to cash in the Fixed Income class – this is my preference as well.

The two other asset classes that are commonly used are Real Estate and Alternatives. The Real Estate class can refer to physical property, such as a house, tract of land, office building, apartment complex...but it also can contain mutual funds that buy companies that in turn buy these things. A beginning investor will probably want to stick to the latter.

Alternatives, which a lot of professionals don't even consider a legitimate investment asset class (but I do), can contain things such as commodities (gold, silver, platinum), natural resources (oil and gas, for example), sometimes even hedge funds....pretty much anything that does not fall into one of the first three categories often gets lumped into this one.

Since this book was written specifically for people just starting to build their financial life, I'm only going use Equity and Fixed Income as asset classes throughout the rest of this book. It's not uncommon for investment professionals to include real estate mutual funds in with the Equity class, since most of them buy stocks of *companies* that buy real estate anyway. And it's unlikely at this point in your life you'll want to do much in the Alternatives space anyway.

For those that are interested in these other types of investments, I'm planning a follow-up to this book on advanced investing techniques, and I'll also discuss them on the Building Lifetime Wealth website from time to time.

So Equities and Fixed Income it is. Within each of these two (as well as the two we're leaving out), we can break down the investments they contain into smaller sub-sections, that will allow us to get a much better idea of how diversified we really are as well as what levels of risk and expected reward are involved in our portfolio. These sub-sections are known as Style Categories. Also, since this section is about mutual funds, that's how we'll frame the discussion about the various categories available.

Mutual funds are run by a person known as the manager, or, more commonly these days, a group of people known as the management team. The manager or management team decides what stocks or bonds to buy and sell for the fund's portfolio. Most mutual fund managers have created an investment process around their particular skills and expertise. Funds that are run by group of managers typically have built a team that shares a common investment philosophy, and a common approach to investing. This process, philosophy, and approach is known as the mutual fund's *style*.

Investing style, when it comes to **equity mutual funds**, is commonly looked at in two dimensions, or along two different scales. The "scales" look at the characteristics of the types of stocks the fund manager prefers to invest in. These two dimensions are:
- Company size
- Value (price of the stock) vs. growth (the company's future growth prospects)

To understand this concept better, it might be helpful to look at it graphically. Then we can define further what each dimension is and what goes into the categories within each. To do this, we'll look at a **Morningstar Style Box**. Morningstar is the world's premier mutual fund data-gathering service, and to help analysts and investors better understand the style characteristics of the thousands of mutual funds available in the U.S., they created this grid:

	Value	Blend	Growth
Large			
Mid			
Small			

Now let's define the dimensions more, and then you'll be able to see how useful this grid can be.

Value vs. Growth

When it comes to stock-picking philosophies and strategies, there are two large schools of thought. One group tries to find stocks that are selling below what they believe its fair price is. They calculate what they see as the "intrinsic value" of the stock based on the company's financial condition and other data, and when they find a stock that is trading below its company's intrinsic value per share, they consider buying it. When stocks they already own start trading above intrinsic value, they usually sell it. These investors are looking for stocks they see as good values for money, hence, the are called *Value* investors.

Another group ignores (or mostly ignores) what prices stocks are selling for, and looks for companies with very strong growth prospects. These companies are usually on the cutting edge of innovations within their industry, or have some kind of catalyst that will lead to above-average growth. This could be sales growth, earnings growth; there are a number of factors these types of investors look at to see whether a company can grow faster than its competitors. They are even willing to pay more for a stock than they think it might be currently worth, because they believe a fast-growing company will lead to a fast-growing stock price. These types of investors, not surprisingly, fall into the *Growth* camp.

If you look at the Morningstar Box above, you'll see a "Blend" column. Not every mutual fund's process fits neatly into one style category or another. Also, to assess which mutual fund belongs where, Morningstar makes a judgement on every stock, as to whether it is a "value" or "growth" stock. Sometimes, what Morningstar might consider to be a Growth stock could be looked at by a mutual fund manager as a Value stock, and be purchased by a Value manager. This can lead to funds being catagorized outside of the box the manager's process might otherwise put them in.

There's another group of mutual funds that do not fit into either the Value or Growth boxes. These funds are run by managers who adhere to both philosophies. They're looking for fast-growing companies, but are not willing to overpay for their stocks. These funds are referred to as having a *Growth at a Reasonable Price* process, also known as GARP. Many of these funds will fall into that middle Blend column in the Morningstar grid.

You may be thinking that all of this sounds a bit imprecise. If that's what you're thinking, you're right! This is one of those art-vs-science elements to investing. The Morningstar Style Box is not perfect, but for beginning investors it's a great tool to have. It's even very useful for professional analysts, though usually as a starting point for further study. If you don't have the time or experience to dig deeper into a fund's style, then it's fine to use the Morningstar classification of a fund *as is*.

Company Size

The second dimension of equity mutual funds' styles, company size, is a lot more clear-cut than the value-vs-growth argument. Though it's not a perfect measurement either. Here's how it works:

Every stock in a mutual fund's portfolio has its ***capitalization*** level calculated. Capitalization is simply the size of the company based on its stock price and the number of shares it has outstanding. These two data points are multiplied together, and that's the stock's capitalization. Nothing to argue about there; very precise.

You'll see the Morningstar grid has 3 rows for company size: Large, Mid, and Small. Here is where each company will fit in based on its capitalization (also called Cap Size):

- Large: above $10 billion
- Mid: between $2 and $10 billion
- Small: below $2 billion

But that's not the end of the story. Many mutual fund managers will only consider buying companies of a certain size – these funds are easy to fit into one of the size rows. But other managers don't care so much about the size of the company as they do whether it meets their style criteria (value or growth). That's where putting the fund into one of the boxes becomes murky. Morningstar typically classifies a fund based on the average cap size of the company in the fund's portfolio. Most of the time, this is a good enough assessment, and for beginning investors, you can use this at face value. Stay tuned for a deeper look into this in the Advanced Investing book coming soon, as well as on the Building Lifetime Wealth website.

So, using the above two dimensions, every equity mutual fund can be placed into one of the 9 boxes on the Morningstar Grid. We'll discuss how to use this in constructing portfolios in the next section.

Bond Mutual Funds

Not to be left behind, bond mutual funds also have their own Morningstar style grid. And here it is:

	Limited	Moderate	Extensive
High			
Medium			
Low			

This grid isn't as straightforward as the equity version, so I'll just explain it on a basic level (which is really all you need to know about it at this point). Across the top, funds are evaluated based on how sensitive the bonds in their portfolio to changes in interest rates. I don't know about you, but I feel a headache coming on just thinking about what that might mean! So, we can look at it a much simpler way. Short-term bond funds will fall into the column of the left, long-term bonds on the right, and intermediate-term bonds in the middle. More on that when we talk about building investment portfolios.

The vertical axis of the grid is a lot easier to understand and a lot less nebulous. The three designations refer to the average credit quality of the bonds the fund holds. In general, the High row is reserved for funds that hold bonds with an average rating of AA and above, Medium covers the AA- to BBB- space, and Low is reserved for non-investment grade bonds (below BBB-). This isn't an exact science, because for one thing some bonds are not rated, and a rather complicated formula is used to arrive at a weighted average for each fund. But in general Morningstar does a very good job of putting bonds funds into their proper category, so I recommend just going with their assessment.

Other types of Mutual Funds

I mentioned earlier that there is a group of mutual funds that is (or tries to be) more diversified than your standard equity or bond mutual fund. I also said I don't recommend them, but they do exist (and are usually available as an option in most 401k plans), so I'll spend a little bit of time talking about them before we move on to actually building portfolios.

Some mutual funds contain both stocks and bonds. The reason for this is that the manager (or fund company) is trying to add value by setting the proper mix of stocks and bonds in a portfolio, rather than you having to do it yourself in your overall portfolio. There are two types of these funds aimed specifically at helping you save for retirement:

Target Risk and Target Date funds.

A number of mutual fund companies offer what are called "Target Risk" mutual funds which are in many 401(k) plan lineups. These funds have names such as "Aggressive", "Conservative", "Balanced", "Moderately Aggressive", etc., with the thought being that you can match your goals and/or your mindset to the proper fund. So if you are willing to take on a lot of risk, you might choose the "Aggressive" fund, or if you're not willing to take much risk at all, you would choose the "Conservative" option, and so on. The point of these funds is that you don't have to do any of your own work in picking investments, you just make one choice based on your mindset, and let the managers do the work for you.

There's another group of similar funds that are growing rapidly in popularity called "Target Date" funds. These are even easier to choose than Target Risk funds, because you just match the approximate year you expect to retire (figuring that you will retire somewhere around age 65, usually) to the fund with an appropriate year in the title (for example, if you think you will likely be ready to retire in the year 2058, and one of the options is the XYZ Target Retirement 2060 fund, that's the one you would choose). These funds are typically offered with retirement years spanning every 5 years (2025, 2030, 2035, 2040, etc.). What could be easier?!

And, as an added benefit, target date funds change their allocation between stocks and bonds so that the funds become more conservative as the target retirement date approaches. This follows standard asset allocation theory, and is something a great many investors that choose their own individual investments tend to do as well.

I'm not going to tell you that these are bad funds, or the concept itself is bad; they have helped many, many investors save for retirement much more easily than they otherwise would have. And if you are unwilling or unable to put any more effort or research into choosing investments, then these funds are an outstanding idea.

But since you bought this book, you probably want to know more about finance and investments than just picking one mutual fund and calling it a day. So before I show you how to build your own portfolio, I'll tell you why I'm not a huge fan of Target Risk or Target Date funds:

The idea of having your portfolio consist of one fund that does everything for you sounds convenient, and as I said has worked for many investors, but I just don't believe that having one investment in your portfolio makes you well-enough diversified. For one thing, you are exposing your portfolio to the risk that the manager of the fund you choose will pick bad investments, even if he gets the mix of stocks-to-bonds right. That risk exists with every actively-managed mutual fund, of course (see Active vs Passive below for more details), but when you have more than one fund in your portfolio, you spread this risk around a bit! If you have 10 funds and 1 fund's manager goes off the rails, you have 9 other funds to prop up your investment money.

To combat this problem, some people mix Target Date or Target Risk funds with standard stock and/or bond funds. If you do this, you're defeating the whole purpose of letting the fund's manager choose the proper asset mix for you! How do you know how much your total portfolio has in stocks and in bonds? You can find out, but it's going to require a lot more analysis than you're likely to want to do, and you would be aiming at a moving target anyway.

Another problem unique to Target Date funds: they take you into the realm of one-size-fits-all, which I am rarely if ever an advocate of. You get the same mix of stocks and bonds as every other investor in the fund regardless of how much risk **you** are comfortable taking. Imagine going to a restaurant and ordering steak, but instead of the waiter asking you how you would like it cooked, something is just plopped down in front of you several minutes later. If you like your steak medium-rare, and you basically get a lump of charcoal on your plate, you're not going to be too happy. Or if you prefer well-done, and the steak is still mooing as it's placed in front of you, you probably won't be returning any time soon. But that's what you get when you buy a Target Date fund: the level of risk the manager wants you to have, not what you feel comfortable taking on.

So my recommendation, for readers of this book, is to avoid Target Risk and Target Date funds. Which is a timely piece of advice, because now we'll discuss how you can put together a well-diversified portfolio that will meet your needs and goals without becoming a professional investment analyst!

Building an investment portfolio

OK, so you're ready to build a portfolio! What is a portfolio? A portfolio is a group of assets that is put together for a reason: to achieve a goal, to showcase the value of the assets, to help analyse them better... or a combination of these and other reasons why it makes sense to look at things as a group rather than just individually. And a portfolio can consist of anything of value: not just stocks or bonds, but also potentially houses, coins, photos (if you're a model for example, which...would not apply to me). Since this chapter is about investing however, we'll keep our discussion to investment portfolios.

Why look at our investments as a group, or a portfolio? To make it easier to know exactly what we have, and whether we have the right mix and depth of investments to meet our needs and reach our goals. We need to know things like:

- Do I have the proper level of exposure to all of the types of assets and style categories I need to achieve my goals?

- Am I taking on more risk that I'm comfortable with (or less risk than I need in order to earn the amount of reward I need)?

- Are there any components to my holdings that are not doing their job: giving me the level of reward they should based on their amount of risk?

So what we need to do from time to time is not only look at each of our individual holdings, but also at our portfolio as a whole. I've already said you don't need to be a professional investment analyst do to this, nor will I try to turn you into one. We'll go over the basics of portfolio construction as well as some key things you should look at to keep your investments on track and your goals achievable.

Asset Allocation

I've already mentioned Asset Allocation a few times, so what is it? Well, it's how you allocate you assets, right? Yes, but...

Of course there's more to it than that. In fact, how you allocate your assets has the biggest impact on what your ultimate investment results will be. Many studies have shown that Asset Allocation accounts for 80-90% of most portfolios' long-term returns. That leaves 10-20% for things like picking stocks, bonds and mutual funds, along with plain old-fashioned luck.

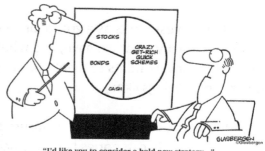

"I'd like you to consider a bold new strategy..."

So getting your Asset Allocation right is extremely important. To do this, we go back to our earlier discussion about risk and reward. You will want to set an overall investment Asset Allocation to match the level of risk you are willing to take. But reward is also part of the equation – you have goals you want to reach, maybe even shorter-term financial needs to be met. So how do you balance the two?

Balance is the right word for it. What's the best case scenario: you take no risk but invest in something that makes you rich quickly, right? It's possible you could get rich quickly: you could go buy a lottery ticket (minimal risk in terms of dollars, you could spend as little as $1, but lots of risk in the sense you could easily lose 100% of your money very quickly), and win the grand prize (huge reward)! But, of course, the chances of that are extremely, extremely small. And it's certainly not an investment strategy, even though some people seem to treat it like it was!

Unfortunately, when it comes to Asset Allocation, there is no absolute perfect answer. There's no formula you can plug numbers into, and have it tell you your best allocation is 68.4% stocks and 31.6% bonds, for example. Just like everything else when it comes to finance and investing, it's part art and part science.

But that doesn't mean you can't set the right allocation for you: you can, even if it is not a precise science. And the best asset allocation for you may change over time, so it's something you will want to look at periodically.

To get started, it might be helpful to ask yourself a few questions. There's no magic to these particular questions, they're just ideas to help you think about how much risk you might be willing to take.

- What is the purpose of your investment account? Are you saving for retirement, do you intend to pull money out of the account as you need it, or is this money you are willing to set aside for the long-term?

- Will you be using money you can afford to lose if necessary, or is this money you need to pay bills with (see Investing vs "Play" Money, below)?

- Does it make you upset when you see your account balance go down every once in a while, or are you able to ride out and ignore short-term fluctuations in the value of your account?

- Is this money you intend to live on someday?

The point of asking yourself questions like these is to figure out the following:

- Are you in this for the long-term or short-term?

- What is your tolerance for risk (see risk tolerance, above)?

- Are you using money you have set aside to invest, or is this "play" money?

Investing vs "Play" Money

Before we go any further with constructing your portfolio, let's talk about what kind of money you're going to use to get started.

I've talked a little bit about "Play" money: no, I don't mean Monopoly money or something that has Donald Trump's picture on it. The difference between investing money and play money is whether you can *afford* to lose it if something goes wrong.

Of course, you could potentially always lose all of your money in any kind of investment, if things go terribly awry. But play money is money you truly don't need; you wouldn't miss it if it were all gone. This is the kind of money that, if you're a gambler, you take to the casino. If you're smart, you've already in a sense written it off. It's gone. If any is left at the end of the day, it's a bonus. That's why it's called play money: you can play with it and not have it affect your lifestyle if you lose it.

When it comes to investing, it's also not a bad idea to separate your funds into what I call "serious" money, and the aforementioned "play" money. Of course, you can only do that if you actually have an amount of money you can afford to "play" with! Otherwise, it's all serious money.

But if you do want to use some money to "play" with, or to "speculate" (see investing vs speculating above), or to purchase risky investments, that's fine, in fact, if you can do it, it's great! Maybe you've read about some small up-and-coming company recently, and you want to buy a few shares of its stock. You know it's risky....so you use some of your play money to buy the stock. Absolutely nothing wrong with that! The points I want to make here are:

- If you want to invest (and please do!), use your investing, or serious money. If you want to speculate, or even buy investments that have tons of risk, use your play money.
- Never put money into either category, investing or play, that you need to pay bills with, buy food with, or that will cause you financial problems if you no longer have it.

The above points should be pretty obvious, but casinos are pretty large and impressive because, for one reason, too many people have brought their rent money to the blackjack table and lost it. Don't do something similar when it comes to investing, please.

Back to Asset Allocation

OK, so you have a pool of money you want to invest, you've figured out how tolerant you are to take on risk, and now it's time to start allocating your account. As I've said a few times already, there is no magic to this: it's part art, part science, like most of investing is. But you also don't need to guess; I'll give you a few guidelines to help you set something useful and meaningful.

Also as I said earlier, in this book we're just going to look at asset allocation as choosing a mix of stocks and bonds, or equity and fixed income. The following chart might help you choose an asset allocation, though I'm also providing it as an *example* of how I see different mindsets and risk tolerances correspond to possible allocation levels:

Investment Mindset	% allocated to Equities	% allocated to Fixed Income
Extremely Aggressive	100	0
Aggressive	80-90	10-20
Moderately Aggressive	70	30
Balanced	50-60	40-50
Moderately Conservative	40	60
Very Conservative	20-30	70-80
Extremely Conservative	0-10	90-100

If one of the mindset descriptions matches you, and you like the corresponding asset allocation, use it! Here is another approach, if you prefer this method:

Since the target audience for this version of the book is the 18-25 age range, I consider a "balanced" asset allocation for this group to be 60% Equities / 40% Fixed Income. So let's start there. Then let's make a few adjustments based on the following:

- Did you set up your account for the long-term? In other words, do you plan on keeping most or all of the money in the account (except in the case of emergencies) until you get close to retirement? If so, I would add around 10 percentage points to the equity allocation that we started with of 60%. If not, if you plan to be taking money in and out frequently, subtract 10 or so from equities. If you're not sure, don't make any change to your allocation yet.

- Will it upset you if you see your account balance fluctuate on a daily basis, or are you able to ignore the short-term ups and downs and focus on the long -term? If the first part applies to you, subtract another 10% from equities, otherwise add 10%.

If you're somewhere in between, keep the allocation as it was after the first question above.

- Will you lose sleep over the prospect of losing money? I know this is similar to the question above, but think of this as maybe going through a 2-3 year slump rather than looking at things day to day. If you don't like the thought of risk, subtract another 10-20 percentage points from equities. If you rather like the prospect of higher risk giving you the potential for higher long-term reward, you might want to add 10-20 points to your equity allocation.

Whichever approach you use, hopefully now you have a good idea of how much you should allocate to equities, and how much to fixed income. Don't forget, your allocation has to add up to 100%! One last recommendation: I would avoid an allocation of either *all* equities or *all* fixed income. For most people, your accounts should contain at least some of each type of asset. So, referring to the allocation table above, I wouldn't go above 90% when it comes to equity allocation, nor would I go below 10%.

Changing your allocation

Just a few quick notes on when to change, and when not to change your asset allocation. As I've said elsewhere in this chapter, I recommend looking at your asset allocation along with the individual investments you've chosen, at least once a year as well as whenever you have a significant life change. A better plan is to look at everything once every 3 months, but it's up to you based on your time and interest level in investments.

Here is when to consider changing your asset allocation:

- There has been a major event in your life that has caused you to be more risk tolerant, or less so. Maybe you are having financial problems and feel it's right to be a little more cautious with your money. In this case you might want to decrease your exposure to equities, and increase your fixed income allocation. If your income has increased significantly, and you now feel that you can take more risks for the prospect of higher returns, then it's ok to add to your equity allocation, and decrease your fixed income exposure.

Here is an example of when **NOT** to consider changing your asset allocation:

- The stock market has been going way up lately, and you have a hunch it's going to come back down soon. Or visa versa. Please, leave your asset allocation alone. Making changes based on what you "think" might happen soon in the market is called Market Timing, and it's always a bad idea. Invest for the long-term, and ignore short-term (even year-to-year) market swings.

That's the message I want to leave you with when it comes to asset allocation. Pick an allocation based on your mindset and life circumstances, and stick with it until something significant happens in your life to change your long-term goals and needs. Otherwise, please leave it alone!

Picking individual investments

So if Asset Allocation determines 80-90% of a portfolio's long-term gains, does it really matter what investments you choose? Yes, very much so! How many races would you win if you only ran 90% of the way to the finish line? If you only finish 80% of an exam, what's your grade going to look like? That 10-20% can, and likely will be, the difference between good and poor investment performance.

As I've said, there are many things you can put into a portfolio, even an investment portfolio. In this book, I will only talk about stocks, bonds and mutual funds – I will cover other types of investments on the book's website, and even in future books. In fact, let's eliminate individual bonds from this list too. I certainly do not recommend beginning investors (nor most experienced investors for that matter) pick their own individual bonds. Of course you will want to have bonds in your portfolio, but I suggest you do so in the form of bond mutual funds.

I'm also not going to talk about picking individual stocks in this book (sorry!). This topic will be discussed in upcoming books in the Building Lifetime Wealth series as well as on the website.

But I would like to say one thing about individual stocks before getting into how to pick mutual funds. Please, if you are going to pick individual stocks, diversify your portfolio!

Diversification

I'm sure you know a little bit already about what diversification means ("don't put all of your eggs in one basket"), so I'll spend more time talking about why it's important rather than defining it. I'll just say that when it comes to an investment portfolio, diversification involves buying assets of different types so that if something goes wrong with one particular investment (or group of similar investments), your entire portfolio won't necessarily be harmed.

Since this section is about individual stocks, I'll talk about diversification with respect to those, and later address how to diversify among mutual funds. If you're going to pick your own stocks, and there's enough discussion on that elsewhere in this chapter so I won't repeat it here, at least do yourself a huge favor: unless you are just getting started in the market, and don't have enough money yet for a diversified portfolio, don't put all of your money in one stock!!

"Diversify, diversify, diversify. Never keep all your eggs in one basket, unless it's Easter."

Let me explain a little bit about what I just said. While I believe a diversified portfolio of assets is the only way to succeed over the long-term when it comes to investments, I also do not think it's a bad idea to start out with just one stock. Or even two. I think this is a great way to learn about investing and the markets, and now with phone apps that make trading cheap (no commissions!) and easy, if you're young and getting started, but all means buy one stock! But your goal, hopefully within a year or two and when you have more money to invest, really should be a diversified portfolio of the kind that I talk about in this book and on the website.

That said, and without getting too deeply into it, here's a little bit about the broad risks you face when buying stocks, and why it's important to eventually diversify your holdings:

- There's an inherent risk in buying stocks in general. No matter which stocks you buy, stocks as an asset class carry a unique amount of risk, just as all types of assets do. For now, we'll call this Market Risk, or the general risk of being in the stock market (this is also known as Systematic Risk).

- There's an additional level of risk associated with each individual company you buy the stock of. This type of risk applies to one particular company, or even a particular industry, but not all companies in general. Some of these risks come from company or industry events that might occur, such as:
  - A strike that shuts down a factory
  - A natural disaster that befalls a particular company's facilities
  - The CEO of the company is killed in a plane crash
  - The price of a certain input (for example, rubber, oil, cheese, etc.) rises

There are many types of events than can affect a company or industry such as this, that would have absolutely no effect on a different company or industry (or might even benefit competitors). We call this Company-Specific (or Unsystematic) Risk.

There's good news when it comes to Company-Specific Risk: you can get rid of it! The more different, and I do mean different, companies' stocks you purchase, the lower the Company-Specific Risk within your portfolio becomes.

I'm often asked how many stocks a person needs to have in their portfolio to be truly diversified. I'll cover this in a lot more depth in future books, but for now, I'll point to the results of many studies on the subject that have shown great risk-lowering, diversification benefits to adding one more stock to a portfolio that start to taper off after about the 10th stock. My recommendation is, if you want to build a portfolio of individual stocks, you have at least 10-20 stocks in your portfolio, unless you will have a blend of individual stocks and stock mutual funds, in which case 10 might be a good number.

Remember at the beginning of this section how I said you want different *types* of stocks in your portfolio? If you buy 20 stocks, and they are 20 different oil drilling companies, or 20 different drug makers, you're not at all diversified. You'll want stocks in a number of different industries, that do a number of different things and make different types of products, or provide different types of services. That way, if the price of oil plunges, or the price of cheese skyrockets, or there's a sudden widget shortage, no more than 1-2 of your stocks suffers rather than all 10-20.

As always, you can find more on this very important topic on the book's website.

Mutual fund portfolio

Building an investment portfolio is not an either/or proposition when it comes to individual securities and mutual funds; it's perfectly acceptable to have a mix of each. However, just for now, I'll talk about mutual fund portfolios as if there was nothing else but funds in them. And then I'll show you how to analyze your overall investment holdings.

Just as there are different types of mutual funds based on what kind of investments they each buy (for example, stock mutual funds, bond mutual funds, etc.), there's another key distinction you need to know about before we talk about constructing actual portfolios: and that is the ongoing active vs. passive debate.

Active vs Passive

What sounds more exciting to you: a) active or b) passive? Which of *these* sounds more exciting: a) watching your money grow, or b) watching it grow faster with less risk? Confused?

You probably picked "a" and then "b"… unfortunately in the mutual fund universe those two answers don't go together. Here's why:

When it comes to mutual funds, Active vs. Passive refers to styles of management. A fund that has an "active" management style means that the **manager or managers are making choices** about what stocks or bonds to buy and sell with their investors' money. A "passive" fund is run by a fixed set of rules that determines which stocks or bonds to buy or sell: the manager(s) **do not make any choices** themselves when it comes to investment decisions.

Let's look at some examples. We'll start with the fictitious PDQ Large Cap Value fund, which is run by a single manager (by this I mean one manager, not that he/she isn't married!). The manager has a team of well-trained analysts who read and examine the financial statements of many large companies; they talk to the management teams of these companies, and basically know how they operate inside and out.

These analysts provide the manager with periodic reports so that the manager can *make informed decisions* about which stocks to buy, and which to give a pass. In addition, these reports help the manager decide whether to hold onto or sell the stocks that are already in the portfolio. The key here is that there is a human being deciding what to buy, hold and sell (much more on the mechanics of mutual fund decision making will be available on the book's website). This is clearly an Active fund.

Now we will look at the equally fictitious ABC Russell 1000 Index fund (the Russell 1000 is an index of large cap stocks). It too has a manager, but he does not have a team of analysts digging through financial statements and providing reports on stocks. Instead, he makes sure that the fund's portfolio contains all of the stocks in the Russell 1000 index in as close of a proportion as possible as to how they are represented in the index. He does not choose stock A over stock B: if it's in the index he buys it, if not, he doesn't. He makes no decisions whatsoever. This is a Passive fund.

The first fund sounds a lot more interesting than the second one, doesn't it? Yes, but...read on before you shun fund #2 in favor of the first one (or you might actually want both in your portfolio). Passive funds (or passive investing) are growing by leaps and bounds, much more so than active funds, largely because of one interesting fact: studies have shown that, in many style categories, 90% of active managers fail to keep up with their benchmarks (see more below on benchmarking). A benchmark is just an objective target that makes it easier to tell whether something is performing well or not.

With mutual funds, the "benchmark" is an index that matches, as closely as possible, the pool of stocks (or bonds) from which the manager(s) draw(s) to build the portfolio. It should also match the manager's investment style (in other words, if the manager buys large cap value stocks, he or she should be evaluated against a large cap value index).

Even in style categories where managers tend to perform better relative to their benchmarks, the "failure to keep up" rate is still around 80%. Why is this? It's because of the Efficient Market Theory, an ongoing discussion of which you can find on the book's website.

So am I saying to never buy actively-managed mutual funds? No, I'm not saying that: it a choice you will eventually have to make as you gain more experience in investing. I own some active funds in my portfolio. But if around 90% of these managers underperform...well, it means that at least 10% of the active managers out there do have long-term performance that is ahead of their benchmark.

The question now becomes whether it's possible to figure out who is in that 10% sweet spot of outperformance. Well, just look at the performance numbers, no? No! It's true you can see whether a manager has outperformed the benchmark over the past 5 or 10 years on any number of dozens of websites that track and report on such things. But does finding a "winning" manager over the past 10 years mean he, she or they is/are bound to continue to beat the index over the next 10? It's a good question, and the answer is: not necessarily.

Take the well-publicized example of Bill Miller, one of the greatest mutual fund managers of all time. As manager of the Legg Mason Capital Management Value Trust fund, Mr. Miller beat his benchmark *15 years in a row* (from 1991 to 2005)! This was followed by several sub-par years, with one of the other funds run by Mr. Miller experiencing extremely poor performance in the years following his amazing run of success. So was Mr. Miller's 15-year streak due to luck? Or did he suddenly turn from smart to not-so-smart overnight?

Likely neither. Mr. Miller is one of the greatest investors of all time, so we can rule out the latter possibility. So was it luck? Academic research would say yes (see the website for much more about academic research regarding efficient markets – we won't go any deeper on the subject in this book). Even Mr. Miller said that his streak was about 95% luck, but I think he was being rather modest. As I've said, over the long-term only about 10% of mutual fund managers beat their benchmarks, and studies have also shown that only about 25% of active managers do so in any given year. This makes the odds of such a run of outperformance astronomical. My assessment is that there is much more to Mr Miller's record than luck!

So if there *is* an element of skill to having an investment record of outperformance against benchmarks (and I still say "if" because research casts very strong doubts on it), how do you find the rare managers who can consistently do it? I have bad news for you (though as you'll see, the news isn't all bad): there isn't a scientific way to do it. So, as it always does, it comes back to the art vs. science of investing. But before I tell you why this shouldn't cause you to lose hope in building a successful investment portfolio (on the contrary, be very hopeful!), let's first wrap up our discussion on active vs passive mutual funds.

Why "passive" is a little more exciting than it sounds

Setting aside the question of skill vs luck when it comes to active managers, there are a number of reasons why you should be at least a little excited at the prospect of passive mutual funds, and why you should seriously consider making them a very significant part of your investment portfolio.

To fee or not to fee

The first factor that makes passive investing worth a serious look is cost. Every mutual fund has what is called an **"expense ratio"**, which is the manager's fee to you for managing your money. Many, far too many, investors make the mistake of overlooking these fees, and since you never see them, they are easy to overlook! Of course you can find out the expense ratio of any mutual fund you own or want to buy, and there are laws requiring funds to be very upfront about the fees they charge. But they are a sort of hidden fee, because you are never presented a bill by the mutual fund for its services. Instead, the fee is drawn directly out of the fund's pool of assets

" I'M THE ONLY KID ON THE BLOCK WHOSE PARENTS DEDUCT A 'MANAGEMENT FEE' FROM HIS ALLOWANCE."

every day, and it causes the price per share to be reduced by the amount of the fee.

Now, the existence of these fees is not a bad thing: do you really expect any professional to work for free?! If someone offers to manage your money for free, unless they are a close friend or relative, wouldn't you be a little suspicious and/or worried? I would.

No, the fees themselves are completely understandable; it's the level of the fees that can range from reasonable to outrageous. And this is where the first benefit to passive investing comes into play: the average expense ratios for passively-managed funds is much lower than the average actively-managed fund's fee. In fact, according to **FINRA** (the U.S. government's **F**inancial **IN**dustry **R**egulatory **A**gency), using data from Thompson-Reuters, the average expense ratio of actively managed mutual funds is 1.40%, vs an average of only 0.60% for passive funds. This makes sense if you think about it: passive managers don't make investment decisions, so they don't have to employ lots of analysts the way active managers do – this saves a lot of money, which they pass on to their investors.

Basis Points

Here's a tip that professional investors and managers use: start to think of percentages in terms of "basis points". A basis point is just 0.01%: so when looking at percentages, always go out to 2 decimal places. This will make it easier to understand basis points. So 1.00% is 100 basis points; 0.06% is 6 basis points, etc.. If fund A returned 10.60% to investors in 2016, and it's benchmark gained 10.10%, you can say fund A beat its benchmark in 2016 by 50 basis points (10.60% - 10.10% = 0.50%, or 50 basis points). This will make understanding fees and return data a lot easier understand.

So is the savings of a mere 0.80% (or 80 basis points – see the sidebar on basis points if you're not familiar with this term) really all that important? Yes, especially for most of you reading this book: 0.80% per year really adds up when you consider most of you will be investors for many decades to come!

Another benefit to using passive mutual funds is that you don't have to worry that the manager is going to have a bad year picking investments, or that the manager of a fund that you like leaves, or any of the other factors that could negatively impact an active fund due its reliance on a human being's intervention rather than an automated process.   We call this *manager risk*, and while it isn't completely zero for a passively managed fund (someone that knows what they're doing has to manage the process that matches a passively-managed fund's portfolio to the index it's linked to as closely as possible), it's so low that investment professionals consider it to in fact be zero. Actively-managed funds carry a great deal of manager risk.

Now to throw a little bit of a wet blanket on the rosy picture we're painting when it comes to passive mutual funds: if you buy them, over the long-term you will have no chance of beating the index that they track. So if your goal is to beat the performance of the S&P 500 Index over the next 10 years, and you buy a very good S&P 500 Index fund, you will not reach your goal. Now, you've probably picked an unattainable goal, or at least one that is very difficult to achieve, but you've also put yourself in a no-win scenario. And, for that moment, we will assume that all passive funds track a particular index and try to match its performance, not beat it. This is true for the largest segment of passive funds, called **index funds**, but there is another group of passive funds that does try to beat their associated indexes, and we will get to those in a moment.

Why wouldn't any investment manager, or individual manager, want to have as high of returns (make as much money) as possible? Well I certainly do, and I'm sure you do, but when it comes to index funds, they have a different mission in life, and I said it in the previous paragraph: they are trying to track an index, not beat it. They want to match the returns of the index as closely as possible, and in so doing match the *risk* level of the index as well. In fact, these managers NEVER want to beat the index they are trying to track, because if they do, it means there is something wrong with their process. As an investor, this is one of the rare times you are not hoping for outperformance: if you buy an index fund that finishes a couple of calendar years in a row ahead of its underlying index, for example, instead of sending a note of congratulations and a bottle of champagne to the manager, you should probably look for a different index fund.

Why? Because if the fund is finishing ahead of its index consistently for a while, you can be sure at some point it's going to consistently underperform by just as much. It's not following the index well, therefore it is giving you more volatility, or risk, than you want. This defeats one of the main points of buying an index fund.

The degree to which an index fund is successful or not at matching the returns of its underlying index is measured by a statistic called **tracking error**. This is a key concept in investing, and fortunately it's an easy one to understand, so please keep it in mind. It's used like this: the higher the tracking error, the worse job the index fund is doing at tracking it's index. So when it comes to tracking error of an index fund, lower is always better.

Not all passive funds are index funds

I've spent a fair amount of time talking about how index funds do not want to beat their benchmarks, and neither should you want them to.

But there is a segment of the passive mutual fund world that actually does try to beat its benchmark, and despite what I wrote in the last several paragraphs, you shouldn't necessarily start running away. These funds are passively-managed, but they are not index funds. Since they don't really have a category of their own, I call them – get ready for a really clever name – **non-index passive funds**.

Ok, maybe not the most clever or inventive thing you've ever heard, but it is a very important distinction to make. Too many investors incorrectly think all passive funds are index funds, and evaluate them accordingly. Here's how they work:

Most non-index passive funds start with a specific index. But, instead of just buying all the stocks or bonds in that index in the same proportions they make up of that index, they make some sort of change designed to beat the returns of the index, without raising the risk of the fund by a corresponding amount. So, they are aiming for higher returns, with only slight higher (or the same level of) risk.

Here are a few examples: one fund family (see the book's website to find out which one) typically takes a very large index of stocks, and buys more of the smaller companies' stocks than their weighting in the index (we call this "overweighting"). They also overweight stocks that, put a lot more simply than it really is, they consider a good value (see the value vs growth discussion earlier in this chapter). The reason for this is that academic research has shown that, over a very long period of time, small cap and value stocks have outperformed the rest of the market. So by overweighting these two segments of the market, they believe they can add more return to investors that the index can strictly give them, without adding to risk.

Another fund family uses a similar approach in creating a set of non-index passive funds. Instead of overweighting small companies and value stocks, they give greater weighting in the portfolio to companies that their algorithms tell them are in the most solid financial shape (also known as the most fundamentally sound). Both of these approaches have achieved a great deal of success.

A very important factor to keep in mind when it comes to non-index passive funds: they differ from index funds in that they are not just buying or replicating an index as is, but they are still passive because pre-set standards, driven by computers rather than human judgement, are making the buy and sell decisions (as well as setting each stock or bond's weightings). The key here is that there is no person or team of people saying they prefer stock A to stock B, for example, and making purchase decisions accordingly. If a manager or managers is/are making investment decisions based on their own judgement rather than pre-set rules, then it is no longer a passive fund: it is actively-managed.

I've spend a lot of time talking about the active vs passive divide, because this is becoming more and more of a key factor in investments, and has been for some time. Money flowing into passive funds from investors is greatly outpacing the amount going into active funds. I think there is a good reason for this: academic research has shown that passive mutual funds are the optimal way to invest. But, you can build an outstanding portfolio with some of each, which I will show you how to do shortly.

Before summing up the differences in the great active/passive divide, I'd like to give you a word of caution. Some of the funds which use a very passive investing approach based on the criteria I've given you above (and will recap below) have decided to try to call themselves active. Don't be fooled by this! If a human is making any kind of portfolio decision, it's an active fund, but if everything is rules/algorithm-driven and no human judgement is being used, it's a passive fund. This distinction is important not just so that you can get labels right, but rather because you have to know what you're dealing with to make sure you're getting the levels of risk and reward you expect and think you are getting (and to make sure you are paying the right level of fees).

Here's a summary of the key differences between passive and active management:

Attribute	Passive		Active
	Index	Non-Index	
Fees	Lowest	Higher than Index funds, but still below average	Below average to very high
Human decision making	No	No	Yes
Tracking Error	The lower the better	Not as important	Not important
Return goals	Index only	Slightly above index	Beat the benchmark
Risk level	Lowest	Low	Higher than passive

I'll tell you how this relates to creating portfolios as we move through the rest of this section.

So now let's turn back to the style box discussion from several pages ago. You can use each of the two Morningstar boxes to help select style categories to have represented in your portfolio, based on the asset allocation you've chosen from that section of this chapter.

One note regarding those style boxes: they relate to equities and fixed income as a whole, but what we haven't talked about yet is choosing between US-based companies (domestic) and overseas-based companies (international, or foreign). And international companies can be further broken down based on whether they reside in countries that have large, developed economies (usually called Developed International or Developed Markets), or smaller, less developed economies (called Emerging Markets).

You can use Morningstar's classification when it comes to international mutual funds at face value. Funds that are based in developed economies will fall into style categories such as Foreign Large Value, Foreign Large Blend, or Foreign Large Growth, etc., while funds that buy stocks based in emerging market countries will usually be classified as Diversified Emerging Markets funds. Much, much more on this, as well as which countries fall into which categories, can be found on the book's website.

So how does this upset the equation? My recommendation is to put 20% of your asset allocation to equities as well as fixed income into international funds. If you feel sceptical toward what's going on outside the USA, maybe you might want to cut this down to 10%, or even 0% (I don't recommend going below 10% though). If you feel you have an above-average tolerance for risk, you might want to bump your international allocation up to 25 or 30% of what you've decided to put into equities and fixed income overall.

Back to the style boxes: each grid (the one for equities and the one for fixed income) has 9 boxes, representing 9 different style categories. But you don't necessarily have to have a fund from each box in your portfolio. It's not like you have to check off or put a mark in each box: you're not playing Bingo! First I'll give you my thoughts on the equity box, then we'll turn to fixed income.

If you turn back to the section where I present the Morningstar style boxes, you can see that the equity style grid has a row for Large, Mid, and Small-sized companies. You might want to have a fund in all 3, but here's what I do: I skip Mid altogether. The Mid Cap category contains a lot of funds that are just passing through: either on their way up to Large, or falling down into Small. I just focus on the Large and Small rows. There's nothing at all wrong with Mid Cap stocks or the funds that purchase them, but I try to keep the number of funds in my portfolio to a reasonable level, so that's why I just have Large and Small Cap funds.

So that leaves 6 boxes to fill. What I do with those boxes is just a matter of personal taste: I tend to use actively-managed funds for the Value and Growth columns, and index funds in the middle Blend column. When it comes to International funds, I stick to Large Cap only (just as a risk control measure – there's certainly nothing wrong with picking funds that buy smaller International companies; this is just my preference).

Here's what my equity allocation looks like when broken down by style category (I use a 70% equity / 30% fixed income asset allocation:

Large Value	1 Active fund with a 5% weighting
Large Blend	2 Passive funds: 1 Total Stock Market index fund with a 10% weighting, and 1 Non-Index passive fund with a 5% weighting
Large Growth	1 Active fund with a 5% weighting
Small Value	1 Active fund with a 5% weighting
Small Blend	2 Passive funds: 1 index fund with a 5% weighting, and 1 Non-Index passive fund with a 5% weighting
Small Growth	1 Active fund with a 5% weighting
Large Foreign Blend	1 Passive index fund with a 10% weighting; 2 Active funds with a 5% weighting each
Emerging Markets	1 Active fund with a 5% weighting

When it comes to fixed income, I use far fewer funds. I completely avoid the short and long-term bond columns, and just stick with the middle Intermediate-Term bond column. You might want to use more funds than I do; you might some Government Bond funds, or maybe a short-term bond fund if you're on the risk-averse side. Again, here's my lineup:

1 Total Bond Market index fund with a 15% weighting
1 Active Total Return Bond funds with a 10% weighting
1 Active High Yield Bond fund with a 5% weighting

And that's my entire mutual fund portfolio. I want to point out very strongly that there is no magic to this allocation: I'm not suggesting you use the same one or recommending this particular lineup in any way. I showed it to you as a guideline to see what a potential portfolio might look like.

Whatever asset and style allocation you want to create, I suggest you use the Morningstar Style Grids as a guideline to help make sure your portfolio is well-diversified. If you want to have a fund in each box on each grid, that's fine. I don't, but it doesn't mean you can't or that there's anything wrong with doing it that way.

But whatever allocation you choose, whichever style categories you want represented in your portfolio, please diversify as much as possible. Eventually I think you will want to have a minimum of 10 mutual funds in your portfolio, and probably more as time goes on.

However, when you're just starting out, you might not have enough funds to spread around to 10 different mutual funds. That's perfectly fine! In that case, I suggest you start with just 3 types of funds:

- A Total Stock Market index fund
- A Total International Stock Market index fund
- A Total Bond Market index fund

As your investing pool grows, you can then (if you wish) add actively-managed funds around the original "core" of index funds you used to get your wealth-building account started. I would suggest leaning more toward passive funds than active funds, for reasons I've probably already spent enough time discussing in this book.

I will talk a lot more from time to time on the book's website and in future books about asset and style category allocation. But for now, I hope the above information will help you on your way to a well-diversified portfolio that matches your appetite for risk and sends you on your way to achieving your financial goals and dreams!

Which funds to choose?

Ah, now we're in the realm of a topic that even professionals struggle with: which funds do I choose to fill out the allocations I've decided on?

Unfortunately there just isn't room in this book to cover all of the principles and techniques used in investment analysis. Otherwise it wouldn't be **a** book, it would be a series of textbook-sized volumes! That's why I address this in much greater detail in my next several books.

Picking individual investments, whether stocks, bonds, mutual funds or whatever else is, as I've said many times already in this book, part science, part art. There is no set of rules, no perfect formula to choose the perfect investments to fill out your portfolio with.

Many professional money managers, analysts, consultants, advisors, and chief investment officers, will tell you that they have a way to pick future winners; they've found the recipe to the proverbial secret sauce. I've seen many of these systems in action first-hand: they usually involve taking a number of data points from funds' recent history, say anywhere from 10 to 20 (I saw one once that looked at 55 factors), and give the fund a thumbs up if it exceeds some set criteria on 6 or 7 out of 10, or 15 out of 20, etc.

The problem *isn't* that these systems use past data to try to predict future events (as far as I know, nobody has found a way to see into the future yet), because that's all you have to go on. The problem is that few or none of these systems use factors that have solid *predictive* value. That is, there is no evidence that any of the data points these systems use can predict what the funds they analyze will do in the future.

So you can't use the past, and unless you're a time traveller you can't use the future...how do you analyse investments?? Actually you can use the past, you just have to be careful of how you use it. The systems I described above are what are often called "Black Box" approaches, because they try to tell you if you put numbers in, you get a set answer out. So if the systems says a fund has to meet 70% of its criteria, for example, a fund that scores 71% is good, while one that scores 69% is bad. There is a technical term we use in the world of investments for this: hogwash. It also has other names, but I can't really print some of them in a clean, friendly book like this! On the other hand, managers that use a Black Box approach to evaluating funds as a means of narrowing the vast number of funds out there to a small number to subject to further scrutiny...that could actually be an acceptable idea.

So what do you do? I will cover this in great detail in future books. For now, you can do one of two things: make choices yourself, or seek the help of professional money managers to choose funds for you. Either way is fine: there are some outstanding money managers out there, great investment analysts, and fantastic registered investment advisors. But I'm guessing that at this point in your life you might not be able to afford to hire a money manager – that's perfectly fine, I'll give you a few tips in this book, and a lot more in the next one!

It all comes back to Risk and Reward

So how do you take the universe of around 20,000 mutual funds, and come up with a portfolio of just 10? Again, this is a question that perplexes even professionals! It's definitely not an easy task.

The first thing you might try is Morningstar.com. They have quite a few free functions, as well as a premium service which costs about $200 a year. You can probably find most of what you need there for free. Try their mutual fund screening function, and then look at the sections below for what to screen for.

Another idea is to just do a Google search. Type in something like "Top 10 Large Cap Growth funds", or whatever type of fund you're looking for. This is actually not a bad way to generate ideas if you're a beginning investor.

When we get to 401(k) portfolios in the next section, it's a lot easier to create a portfolio since the task of boiling down the entire mutual fund universe to a reasonable number of funds from which to choose has already been done for you. But when you're putting together your own portfolio from scratch... I'll tackle index funds and active funds separately when it comes to this issue:

Index funds

When you buy an index fund, you are trying to gain the risk and reward characteristics of the index – nothing more, nothing less. And you want to do it for as low a cost (expense ratio) as possible. So that means you want index funds that have the:

- Lowest Tracking Error
- Lowest Expense Ratio

The world of index funds is dominated by 3 fund families: Vanguard, Schwab, and Fidelity. So your search for the right index funds for your portfolio should be pretty quick and easy: Look at the funds offered in each category you're looking to fill by these three companies, and make your choice based on the 2 factors I listed above. It doesn't have to be any more complicated than that for you at this point in your investing life!

Actively-managed Funds

I throw non-index passive funds into this category too. Unlike pure index funds, which really do not want to beat the index they are tracking, funds in this category are looking to outperform whatever benchmark they have set for themselves, as well as each other.

As I've said, volumes can be written about investment analysis, but since I'm covering everything in this book at a basic level, I'll just give you a few key things to look for when it comes to actively managed and non-index passive funds:

- Performance. What you are not necessarily looking for here are the funds that have posted the best performance over the past year or two. That can lead to a situation in which you pick funds at their peak, or that have had a lucky year or two and are about to have their luck run out. This is known as "chasing returns", and is a time-tested way to have your portfolio perform very poorly over the long term. A few things you might want to look at (all of this can be found by entering the fund's ticker symbol on Morningstar.com, which will pull up a very nice report you can access for free):
    - Funds that are in the 50th percentile or higher of the peer group over the last 5 years. When it comes to peer group rankings, higher is better.

- Look at the year-by-year returns over the past 10 years. Has the fund consistently outperformed its benchmark and/or peer group average? Or have 1 or 2 really great years been surrounded by 5-6 really bad ones. You want to look for funds that can say yes to the first question, and avoid funds that fall into the second category.

- Risk. And by this, I mean standard deviation. Look at the Risk tab on the fund's Morningstar.com report, and pull up the 5 year standard deviation number. Is it lower than the peer group average number given below the fund's standard deviation? If yes, it's a fund you might want to consider – if not, only choose it if you are looking to build a higher risk portfolio.

- Expense Ratio. Again, you should be able to find the fund's expense ratio along with its peer group average on many websites. Morningstar also rates fund's expenses from High to Low. Look for funds with a Low or Below Average rating.

- Management. Pull up the Management tab on the Morningstar page. It will tell you how long the manager or managers have been leading the fund. Is there 1 manager who has been with the fund at least the past 3 years? If not, you might want to pass on the fund, as all historical data for that fund is meaningless.

You might notice how I've mentioned 5-year data a few times: always use 5-year numbers whenever possible. This way, you have a better chance of catching a full cycle of market ups and downs, and have a better idea of what the fund can do over the long-term. Avoid 3-year data: too many short-term quirks can skew 3-year numbers, and not really give you a clear picture of the fund's true characteristics.

One last thing to look at, or in this case, not to look at. And that is the Morningstar Star ratings. Morningstar gives almost every fund available for purchase a rating of between 1 (bad) and 5 (the best) Stars. However, study after study has shown that this rating system has no predictive value whatsoever. Buying only 5-Star rated funds (and many people do this) is a great way to lead to the "chasing returns" problem I mentioned earlier. The only exception to this is: don't buy a fund with a 1-Star rating. This is the only rating that has consistently been shown to have predictive value. Other than that, ignore the Stars.

My upcoming books will feature much more on picking winning mutual funds!

401(k)s

Building a 401(k) portfolio is a lot easier than building one in a regular investment account, as I've said. And I've already given you the tools to do it! Simply take the available funds in your plan provided to you by your employer, and apply everything I've already talked about in the Mutual Fund portion of this chapter. Apply the criteria in the section above, and choose the funds that are the most attractive based on the applicable criteria. Set your asset allocation in the same manner as for any account as I've described in the Asset Allocation section above. This will enable you to create a solid 401(k) portfolio!

I will just add a one quick thing when it comes to 401(k)s. Almost all of them will offer Target Date and/or Target Risk funds. I've already said I don't recommend them, but I would like to point out that, if you feel more comfortable using them rather than picking your own fund lineup, by all means do so! There are some outstanding Target Date and Target Risk funds available, and while I personally don't use them, it doesn't mean you shouldn't either. Do what makes you feel better about your investment account. There's no right or wrong to whether or not you use these types of funds: it's a matter of personal preference and comfortability. Like most things in the investment world!

However, I would choose between either using Target Date/Risk funds or not using them. Don't create a portfolio that mixes these types of funds with other individual funds you pick on your own.

Conclusion

I sincerely hope this book makes your life a lot easier, that you learned a lot from it, and that it will help you reach your financial goals and dreams. As I've said a few times, I'm planning on a follow-up series of books that will look at investments a lot deeper, and more information will be available, and constantly updated, on the book's website. I welcome all comments and suggestions (there is a place to send them to me on the website, and you're welcome to send me a message on LinkedIn), as I try to give you the most relevant and useful information I can. Best of luck to all of you!

Acknowledgments

While it's impossible to acknowledge everyone who has made a difference in my career and who helped me along the path to getting this book published, I would like to give a special thank you not only to the people I mentioned in the Dedications, but also:

Gina Pellillo, for your support and doing an amazing job of editing and proof-reading; the three cookie-swiping members of my Summer 2017 Finance 311 class, Tina Nguyen, Alyssa Grimaldi, and Maria Trotta, who made the class fun and gave me great support and input on this book; Uliana who has been a great source of support and a good friend for so many years; Dan Crawford for your wisdom, guidance, knowledge and sense of humor; Ken Deutsch, a knowledgeable and consummate investment professional; Brian Fix, the best relationship-manager in the business and another good friend; Nader Khreish, whose humor and friendship made an otherwise intolerable situation tolerable, and whose proofreading expertise I wish I had on this project; Anetia Isbell, without whose wisdom and compassion I'm not sure where I would be in life; Yu Hu, whose wisdom goes well beyond her years and who I think has an amazing future ahead of her; Jeff Doerfler, a top-notch investment professional and one of the best supervisors anyone could ask for; Muning Sun, an outstanding assistant and intelligent young person with a very bright future; the Clement brothers, Jeff, Hank and Steve, some of the very finest human beings you will ever meet; and Allan Fotheringham, who I never met but inspired my writing style nonetheless. If I've left anyone out, I'm truly sorry. I appreciate the guidance, help, and support I've received from all of you.

About the Author

Thomas Rimer is an author, university professor, and financial professional with over 20 years of experience in the investment industry. He is the founder of the Building Lifetime Wealth concept, series of books, and website. These resources are designed to help people of all ages learn about money and reach their financial goals and dreams.

Mr. Rimer has managed money professionally for people ranging from billionaire business owners to coffee-shop baristas, including professional athletes, entertainers, musicians, wealthy retirees, not-so-wealthy retirees, factory workers, and ordinary people from all walks of life. He currently teaches Finance at one of the leading universities in the USA.

Working closely with talented university students, who overwhelmingly have expressed enthusiasm for learning how to manage and invest their money effectively, inspired Mr. Rimer to write this book.

Made in the USA
Middletown, DE
26 October 2023

41402915R00086